Bear-Proof
Investing

Protecting Your Financial Future in a Bear Market and Taking Advantage of an Emerging Bull Market

Kenneth E. Little

ALPHA

A Pearson Education Company

International Standard Book Number: 0-02864204-X
Library of Congress Catalog Card Number: 2001091094

04   03   02   8   7   6   5   4   3   2   1

Interpretation of the printing code: The rightmost number of the first series of numbers is the year of the book's printing; the rightmost number of the second series of numbers is the number of the book's printing. For example, a printing code of 02-1 shows that the first printing occurred in 2002.

Printed in the United States of America

Publisher: Marie Butler-Knight
Product Manager: Phil Kitchel
Senior Production Editor: Christy Wagner
Managing Editor: Jennifer Chisholm
Senior Acquisitions Editor: Renee Wilmeth
Copy Editor: Cari Luna
Cover Designer: Trina Wurst
Book Designer: Trina Wurst
Production: John Etchison, Stacey Richwine-DeRome

For marketing, promotion, or publicity, contact Dawn Van De Keere, marketing manager, at 317-581-3722.

CONTENTS

INTRODUCTION

"What happened?!"

"For years, it was hard *not* to make money in the stock market—all of a sudden, everything is dropping like a lead balloon. Now what do I do?"

That's the question every typical investor is asking after watching dot.coms vaporize, IPOs become DOA, high-tech stocks fizzle, and utilities and blue-chip leaders fall to embarrassing lows.

Over half of all American households have some sort of stake in the stock market, whether through an employer-sponsored retirement plan, employee stock options, or cash in a mutual fund or stock portfolio.

Investing, even in boom times, is never as easy as it may have seemed in the past few years. A bear market makes investment decisions even more complicated. The slide in stock market values began in the second quarter of 2000 and soon became an avalanche. Investors watched retirement dreams change as accounts reversed double-digit growth rates. Younger investors couldn't believe stocks actually went down instead of always up.

The choices facing investors aren't so clear-cut anymore:

- Convert everything to cash?
- Mutual funds?
- Value stocks?
- Real estate?
- Bonds?

Add the voices of the daily business news, which sound like the end of the world is near ("live update at 10"), and it's no wonder investors are confused.

BEAR-PROOF INVESTING

What this book offers you is a set of strategies to make rational decisions about investments in an unstable or down market. These are tried-and-true methods of protecting your portfolio from the worst in falling market conditions.

Your goal in a bear market is to hold your own and position yourself to take advantage of an emerging bull market. In *Bear-Proof Investing*, you will learn ...

- The two most important words in investing.
- The two most dangerous words in investing.
- Economic and market indicators you should watch.
- How to handle short-term financial goals.
- Age-appropriate strategies for retirement planning.
- Safe vehicles for short-term cash reserves.
- How to decide what to hold and what to fold.
- How to fatten your portfolio in a bear market.

Bear-Proof Investing is your edge in an unstable market. It gives you the tools and strategies you need to protect your investments and position yourself to take full advantage of an emerging bull market.

ACKNOWLEDGEMENTS

I would like to thank to Renee Wilmeth, Phil Kitchel, Christy Wagner, and all the other folks at Alpha Books for their hard work in making this book possible. In addition, thanks to my family for letting me shut the door to my office for weeks on end so I could finish this book.

PART 1

BEAR SIGNS

It's easy to spot a bear market, and any other market phenomena, in the rearview mirror. In retrospect, it's easy to see all the warning signs and wonder why it wasn't obvious at the time. Stock market participants are great at pondering the "what if" questions:

* What if I had bought XYZ at $25 instead of $45?
* What if I had sold XYZ at $50 instead of $5?
* What if the CEO of XYZ weren't in prison now?

The dreaded Y2K disaster failed to materialize at midnight on January 1, 2000. Instead, it popped up in the spring when the Internet stock bubble began its protracted burst. By the time the new millennium truly began in 2001, the stock market was in the grips of a large bear. Many younger investors were shocked to learn you could actually lose money in the stock market.

In Part 1, we'll focus on the history of bear markets and define the different varieties (species) of bear markets. We'll discuss the risks associated with investing, and examine economic and market indicators that foretell a bear market.

CHAPTER 1

BEAR MARKETS

A declining stock market may strike younger investors as something of an oxymoron, like jumbo shrimp or military intelligence. However, it is a fact of life, as any investor who's been in the market for more than 10 years knows.

In this chapter, we will look at ...

- The common definitions of bear markets.
- The history of past bear markets.
- The consequences of bear markets.

At the most basic level, stock prices rise when there are more buyers than sellers and fall when there are more sellers than buyers. So what changes buyers to sellers? How can the history of bear markets help us today and warn of future downturns?

DEFINING A BEAR MARKET

The general, but not universal, consensus is that a bear market occurs when the broad market is down by 20 percent or more from the previous month for a "sustained period of time"—usually two or more consecutive months. Some folks place the decline at 15 percent or more; however, the 20 percent number is more common.

That's the technical definition. What matters to you is that the broad markets, and most likely your portfolio, are dropping like rocks and "investor confidence" is right behind them.

Tip —————————————————————————————

There are always pundits, usually with a service to sell, who warn of dire circumstances ahead. When the respected media, like *The Wall Street Journal* and Morningstar.com, start sounding warnings, that's when you should listen.

MARKET CORRECTIONS

You have to understand the definition of a bear market in order to understand the underlying causes. Bear markets and "market corrections" are not the same. Market corrections are declines of short duration, although they can be severe.

The Standard & Poor's 500 Index (S&P 500) lost some 10 percent of its value in just a few days in October 1997. Investors in that month had to decide if this was a market correction or the beginning of a bear market. Investors who panicked and dumped stocks for "safer" havens like bonds and cash instruments watched the market roar back, which put them in the unenviable position of selling low, then buying high to get back in the market. Investors who rode it out saw continued increases until things began to unravel in the spring of 2000. Of course, they then faced the same question again. This time it was a bear market.

THE PSYCHOLOGY OF BEARS

Bear markets are not just movements of stock prices in a downward direction. They also represent a state of mind in the investing community.

During the roaring bull market of the 1990s, the general mood of investors was that stock prices were going to continue to rise. Your entry point didn't really matter because prices were going up. No rational investor will admit to this mindset, but investor confidence was very strong. No one wanted to be sitting on the sidelines while the markets, particularly the Internet/tech stocks, were flying high.

In a bear market, the reverse is true. Investors expect prices will keep falling and take measures to protect their portfolios. Part of this protection usually means dumping higher risk investments for more stable ones. This pressure to sell only adds to the momentum of a declining market.

It usually takes time and sustained good news for a bear market to reverse itself. As we said, this is one difference between a bear market and a market correction.

THE RECEDING BEAR

A bear market and an economic recession are not the same things. Although many of the same factors cause both, the stock markets do not always move with the economy, nor does the economy always move with the markets.

For example, analysts usually consider low unemployment good for the economy because more people are working and they are buying more goods and services. However, the stock market may view low unemployment quite differently. Low unemployment means employers must compete for workers, causing wages to rise. Rising wage rates may drive down profits.

Investors purchase a stock based on the expectation of future profits. If those future profits are threatened, the stock's price may drop as buyers look elsewhere for growth. Of course, it's not quite that simple. Rising wages can bring on inflation, which is one of the major causes of bear markets.

Plain English
> A **recession** is a decline in the gross national product for two consecutive quarters. The **gross national product** is the sum of all goods and services produced in the United States during a single year and is expressed in dollars.

This is not to suggest there is *no* connection between recessions and bear markets. Sometimes a bear market will lead the economy into a recession (after all, investors are betting on the future). Other times a bull market can appear to lead the economy out of a recession: The 1990s bull market began in the middle of a recession.

The point is that investors should look closely at the factors pushing the markets toward a bear state of mind. We will look at these in more detail in Chapter 3, "Types of Bear Markets."

BEAR HISTORY

Bear markets are part of the history of the stock market. They occur often enough for many observers to include them in an ongoing cycle of boom and bust.

The biggest bear market occurred in the 1929 to 1931 market crash, when the market lost almost 90 percent of its value. This devastating loss of wealth and the accompanying depression shaped our history for decades. It took the deficit spending of World War II to get the market back on a sustained track. However, even that didn't last long. The mid-1950s saw the first modern bear market, the first of nine, not counting the one that began in 2000.

Tip

> Deficit spending spurred the economy by making the U.S. government an active buyer of goods and services to support the war effort. Deficit spending, however, can have the opposite effect when taxes are raised to pay the increasing debt.

The sustained bull market of the 1990s convinced many of the 50 million Americans who own stock that they were on a one-way ride to a comfortable retirement. The 10-year run also convinced many people who had never invested in the stock market before to give it a try. Many were totally unprepared for what happened.

The stock market, led by Internet and technology stocks, was highly overpriced. When investors failed to see the profits they expected from these rising stars, they panicked and began a sell-off that drove prices down dramatically. Uncertainty spread to other parts of the market, and the bear was loose.

Unfortunately, history has a way of repeating itself at the most awkward times. If they had looked at the following chart of bear markets since the 1950s, they might have been better prepared for what was coming. This chart shows the nine bear markets leading up to the bull market of the 1990s. Many investors might remember the beginnings of a devastating bear market of 1987 and Black Monday, when the market plunged hundreds of points, as the worst in modern history. The chart clearly shows, however, that it was only the *third* worst, and its recovery was much quicker than previous bears.

Dates	Percent Loss	Length (Months)	Recovery (Months)
Aug. 1956 to Oct. 1957	21.6%	14.7	11.1
Dec. 1961 to June 1962	28%	6.4	14.3
Feb. 1966 to Oct. 1966	22.2%	7.9	6.9
Nov. 1968 to May 1970	36.1%	17.9	21.3
Jan. 1973 to Oct. 1974	48.2%	20.7	69.4
Sept. 1976 to Mar. 1978	19.4%	17.5	17.3
Jan. 1981 to Aug. 1982	25.8%	19.2	2.3
Aug. 1987 to Dec. 1987	33.5%	3.3	19.7
Jul. 1990 to Oct. 1990	19.9%	2.9	4.3

Source: Standard & Poor's Corp.

Many observers called the bear market that began in 1973 a "super" bear, in part because it occurred during a period of high inflation and because of the lengthy recovery. Pity the poor soul who had planned to retire during *this* period. After investing for many years, a long, painful bear market takes almost one half of her portfolio's value, and inflation takes a big bite out of the remainder.

Losing one half of your retirement nest egg would be devastating. Could it happen again? It most certainly could.

Caution

> Don't believe the popular notion that "things are different" now and bear markets will not be long-lived or too severe. No one knows that for sure.

A BEAR LESSON

The previous chart makes it all too clear that investing involves risk. (We'll look at this in more detail in Chapter 2, "Investing as a Contact Sport.") If you look at those nine modern bear markets beginning in 1956 and ending in 1990, you will notice that during this 34-year period, investors have struggled with bear markets about 25 percent of the time. Contrast that with the 10-year uninterrupted run of the last bull market, and it's easy to see how investors became overconfident.

This overconfidence, combined with little experience with bear markets, left many investors wondering what hit them. The classic mistake for inexperienced (and even experienced) investors is to watch prices rise in a bull market and buy near the top. Then when the market heads south, they follow the stock down and sell near the low. A "buy high and sell low" strategy is no strategy at all.

Many folks writing about bear markets encourage investors to sit tight and ride out the storm. This may make sense if the investor is 30 years from retiring, but the poor soul we mentioned earlier doesn't have the luxury of riding out a bear market—she can't wait five years to recover her loss. The only way she can meet her immediate needs is to cut her losses as quickly as possible and retreat to safer investments, such as cash and bonds.

The lesson of the modern bear markets is that what goes up can and almost certainly will come down. Investors need to be prepared.

SLAYING BEAR MYTHS

Not all bear markets are the same. In Chapter 3, we'll go over the primary causes of bear markets in detail. However, it is important to slay some basic bear myths before we go any further.

- **Everyone loses in a bear market.** We've defined a bear market as including most of the market leaders, such as the bellwether S&P 500. Not every stock or even every stock sector loses money during a bear market, and there are always stocks that do poorly during bull markets. The cliché that a "rising tide lifts all boats" is not true in the stock market.

Plain English

The **S&P 500 Index** represents 500 of the largest companies in America. It is the most widely used proxy for the whole stock market and is the most widely used index in measuring performance of investments.

- **You can see it coming.** You can't. Bear markets are notorious for disguising themselves. Market corrections, which we discussed earlier, are great decoys for bear markets: You never know when a market correction is going to escalate into a full bear market. In our earlier example of 1987, investors faced a sharp market decline. Was it a market correction that would rebound shortly, or the beginning of a continual decline into a bear market?

In Chapters 4, "Economic Indicators," and 5, "Market Indicators," we will look at some of the indicators investors should watch for bear signs.

- **Bear traps are false signals sent by the market that suggest it is about to reverse course and head up.** A bear trap occurs when a stock drops sharply and panicked investors sell near the bottom, only to watch the stock rebound. The broad market can execute bear traps also. A straight-line drop in prices seldom marks a bear market. Most often, prices will fall, then rebound to a level near the original point, and repeat the pattern over and over. However, the long-term trend is that the rebound never quite regains all the lost ground.

    Casinos use a version of the bear trap on their slot machines. You put in three coins and pull the lever. A ringing sound means you won. However, when you look in the tray, the machine has only returned two coins. This incremental loss doesn't seem as bad as not getting anything back, so you're encouraged to try again. In the stock market, this type of incremental decline is a perfect disguise for a bear market.

- **Bear markets can be averted.** It's preposterous to think we can control the stock market. If we could control the stock market, there would never be any bear markets. Actions can encourage or discourage bear markets (such as interest rates and taxes), but there are no controls. In Chapter 3, we'll discuss the causes of bear markets in more detail. We may even *need* bear markets to bring down stock valuations to more reasonable levels, thus setting up future bull markets.

    The Persian Gulf War caused the bear market that began in 1990. Oil prices escalated along with interest rates. Rising energy prices often lead to inflation. All these factors negatively affect the stock market. Toward the end of the 1990s bull market, the Federal Reserve Board (the Fed) raised interest rates six times and oil prices escalated. Many feel the Fed went overboard in its attempt to cool the economy and precipitated the bear market.

Caution

> The U.S. markets can be affected by more events abroad than just po-
> litical and military unrest. As globalization continues, we will be more
> vulnerable to problems in foreign markets.

- **The Fed is responsible for the stock market.** The Fed is *not* responsible for the stock market, although it watches the market
  closely. Fed pronouncements about the economy and interest rates
  are widely followed by investors. The Fed views its primary responsibility as controlling inflation. As we will learn in Chapter 3,
  inflation is a primary cause of bear markets, but the Fed is more
  concerned with the whole economy. Inflation is deadly to any
  economy and benefits virtually no sector. The Fed of course knows
  that raising interest rates could eventually hurt the stock market,
  but inflation hurts everyone.

BEAR-PROOFING YOUR PORTFOLIO

You can run, but you can't hide from a bear market. The ugly truth investors discovered after the recent bull market ended is that you can and
will lose money at some point if you stay invested for any length of time.
That's the bad news. The good news is that you can protect your portfolio from the worst effects of most bear markets. The trick is knowing a
bear market from a market correction.

RISK AND INVESTING

Despite all the talk about a "new economy," there are fundamental truths
about investing that haven't changed. The first is that investing involves
risk: There is a chance you will lose money. The more you stand to gain,
the higher the risk.

It's ironic that an investing community that watches and benefits
from markets climbing to dramatic heights is shocked when they collapse.
The Nasdaq Composite Index went from over 5,000 to 2,600 is less than
a year. People were shocked and angry. Those same people didn't mind
when the index was up 80 percent the year before!

In Chapter 2, we'll look at the risks associated with investing and how you can protect yourself. Your tolerance for risk should be one of the primary considerations of your investment plan.

LOOKING FOR BEAR SIGNS

Investors should watch a number of market and economic indicators for signs of a bear. Unfortunately, it is not always easy to identify bear markets, because not all bear markets are equal. Interest rates cause some; others find a home during a recession; some are triggered by political unrest or a war that no one saw coming—the invasion of Kuwait (as well as other factors) triggered the bear market of 1990.

Tip

> When you read about the overpriced "market," understand that it doesn't apply to every stock. Even during the super-heated markets of the late 1990s, there were stocks trading at very low valuations. Some were sound companies that simply didn't excite the investing community like the dot.com wonders of the day.

When markets become overpriced, watch out. At least, that's the conventional wisdom. Market observers repeatedly sounded the warning during the 1990s bull market, but if you had heeded the early warnings and retreated to safer investments, you would have missed most of the strongest bull market in history. When the bubble finally burst, pundits were shaking their heads with an "I told you so" attitude. Like the boy who cried wolf too often in the fairy tale, eventually they were bound to be right.

In Chapters 3 through 5, we will look at different types of bear markets and some of the economic and market indicators that may help you spot them coming.

AVOIDING TRAPS

Part 2, "Bear Traps," deals with three difficult issues for investors:

- Market timing, or trying to buy at the absolute low and sell at the absolute peak

- When to sell a stock
- When to sell a mutual fund

Market timing is a disaster waiting to happen for investors who think they are smarter than the market. No one, no matter what they say in their advertising, can consistently call the market correctly, and neither can you. You don't know where the top is and you don't know where the bottom is. (I don't either.) However, there are solid ways to make investment decisions that take the guessing out of the process. Bear markets, as noted earlier, often disguise themselves as corrections or something else.

There are two sides to every investment decision: when to buy and when to sell (although the buy decision seems to capture more attention than the sell decision). Protecting your portfolio may mean moving out of one class of investment and into another. Do you have an exit plan? We will look at the process of selling stocks and mutual funds in detail.

Plain English

Your **portfolio** is simply your basket of investments. It can include stocks, mutual funds, bonds, and cash instruments.

BEAR YOUR ASSETS

You know that diversification is a powerful safeguard against an unstable market. Asset allocation is how you go about that diversification. Many investment professionals maintain that how you allocate your assets is more important than picking the individual assets. As a rule, you want assets split among stocks, bonds, and cash. A number of factors determine how much you should allocate to each.

In Part 3, we will discuss the process of asset allocation and how factors such as the type of bear market and your age change the contents of your portfolio.

BEAR TRACKS

Part 4, "Bear Tracking," takes a look at some strategies from two perspectives: age and time horizon. Our poor soul at the beginning of this chapter who lost one half of her retirement portfolio the year she planned to retire would have benefited from reading these chapters. We will look at short-term strategies in particular, since almost everyone has financial goals that are less than 20 years down the road.

Are bear markets a time to pick up some bargains on decimated stocks? This strategy walks very close to market timing; however, with the proper research, you may find some roses among the thorns.

BEAR DEN

Investors nearing retirement are the most vulnerable to bear markets because they have less time to ride out the storm. What strategies should you use and when? Part 5 discusses the concerns of pre-retirees and follows them through retirement. You worked hard and invested wisely so you could enjoy a comfortable retirement. Don't let a bear market rob you of that goal.

Are there "safe havens" in a bear market? Although there are no completely safe places to hide, you can protect yourself from the worst the bear has to offer.

BEARSKIN RUG

Part 6, "Bearskin Rug," discusses the three major considerations in surviving a bear market and gives some examples of why they are so important. These tools and techniques will help you avoid the worst the bear has to offer. However, there are no "silver bullets" that are guaranteed to kill the bear.

Investing is about risk, and nothing will change that. You can arm yourself with information and education so you can make investment decisions with a reasonable knowledge of their outcome.

CONCLUSION

Bear markets are as much a part of investing as bull markets. Indeed, we may not be able to have bull markets without bear markets. Unless you like ugly surprises, you should be able to identify bear markets and know what they can do to your portfolio. Forewarned is forearmed.

CHAPTER 2

INVESTING AS A CONTACT SPORT

Investors are, by definition, optimists. After all, you're betting the future will be brighter than the present—at least for your investments. When investors talk about risk, they're asking if the risk of the investment is reasonable compared to the potential gain. You cannot separate risk from investing: No investment is absolutely safe.

The safest investment you can make is in U.S. Treasury bonds because they carry the full faith and credit of the U.S. government. If you had bought a 10-year U.S. Treasury Bond in 1990 and held it to maturity, you would have received your money back plus a guaranteed interest payment in the single digits. However, if you had bought a mutual fund that tracked the S&P 500 in 1990 and held it 10 years, you would have received an average 17-plus percent annual return. Your money would have been "safe" in bonds, but you would have missed out on the greatest bull market in history.

Caution

> Structuring your portfolio for maximum safety makes sense late in life when you can't afford losses. However, while you are still accumulating wealth, a very conservative portfolio may be very expensive in lost opportunities.

RISK AND REWARD

You may have a good understanding of risk, but I encourage you to read this chapter as a review and in light of protecting yourself in a bear market.

One positive consequence of the 1990s bull market was that a large number of people got involved in investing who never had before. Internet and high-tech stocks in particular seemed like they could go nowhere but up. Unfortunately, many new investors lacked the tools to fully understand the risks involved. The hysteria associated with initial public offerings (IPOs) led new investors down a path that would ultimately see a number of these companies go out of business or lose 80 or 90 percent of their value.

Plain English

> An **initial public offering** (**IPO**) is the first issue of stock sold to the public by a company. The company retains the proceeds to finance growth. Once the company sells its stock to the public, subsequent sales are between investors, and the company doesn't receive any of the money.

At the height of the Internet stock "bubble," I was producing a Web site for beginning investors. The questions I received by e-mail showed a dangerous lack of understanding on the part of novice investors: "I've been reading about how much money you can make with IPOs, so I thought I'd get in on the action. How much does 10 shares of IPO cost?"

Money poured into the market in unprecedented amounts, and the bubble got larger and larger. Individual investors were encouraged to dump their low-performing investments and hop on the express train to wealth. Those investors who did well were smart enough to get in at a reasonable price and take a profit in the short run (but this is more like speculation than long-term investing). Ironically, the investors who lost the most got into the market, often near the top, thinking they could ride out falling prices by holding on or even buying more as the stock dropped.

A MATTER OF PERCEPTION

Only you can decide what level of risk you can handle without losing sleep. What may seem risky for one investor may not appear that way at all to another investor. Some investors find individual stocks too risky and are more comfortable in mutual funds where there is professional management and diversification. On the average, individual stocks offer a higher potential return than mutual funds. The major risk factors listed later in this chapter have a greater affect on individual stocks. Individual stocks have no protection by diversification unless you buy a number of different issues in different industries. Diversification is your primary defense against risk.

Nevertheless, you know your stomach's tolerance for stress. Pay attention to your consumption of Rolaids. I've heard too many stories of people who talked themselves into risky situations because their neighbor's dentist's brother-in-law had a sure thing.

T i p

> Hot tips are for suckers. The Internet is a breeding ground for "pump and dump" scams where a person will disclose the name of the next Microsoft with the intention of driving up the price so they can sell at a big profit. Many times the company mentioned has no knowledge of the swindle.

AGE AND RISK

Regardless of your personal tolerance for risk, there are times in your life when it is appropriate to take risks and times when it is not. Simply stated, the closer you are to a financial goal, the less risk you should take. As you approach your goal, the window of time needed to recover from a bear market or even a market correction decreases.

Later in the book, we'll spend more time talking about strategies to address the issues of risk, time, and age in structuring your portfolio.

TYPES OF RISK

There are three basic types of investment risk, and any one or a combination can cause a bear market. However, your investments are subject to these risks even if they don't precipitate a bear market. The types of investment risk are the following:

- Economic risk
- Market risk
- Inflation risk

These aren't mutually exclusive—it is possible to experience all three at once. It is important to note that virtually every stock, mutual fund, or bond is subject to one or all of these risks regardless of whether there is a bear market or not.

Tip

When you see a market going crazy over a particular sector (such as technology stocks), a red flag should warn you that eventually this frenzy will end and the sector will collapse.

MARKET RISK

Internet and technology stocks fueled the 1990s bull market, especially toward the end. The market was definitely behind companies that rushed to the Internet and new technology. It was fairly simple to follow the money and see what was hot. Billions of dollars poured into the high-tech/Internet companies. If you had a two-page business plan and a company name that ended in ".com," no matter how outrageous the plan or inexperienced the managers, there seemed to be no end to the line of people wanting to give you money.

However, many of these "new economy" wonders were really only good at doing one thing: eating money. Toward the end, phrases like "burn rate," which refers to how fast a company is going through its cash, began to be part of the dialogue.

The amount of cash the companies consumed was alarming. Even more alarming was the fact that many of the companies would never make a profit. Investors, particularly big institutions and mutual funds, began to see things more clearly. When the market turned on the Internet and technology stocks, it did so with a vengeance. Stock prices plunged and companies ran for cover by looking for a merger with a strong company. You could say that investors woke up toward the end, rubbed their eyes, and said to themselves, "I'll never drink that hype again."

Meanwhile, many companies such as Bank of America and General Motors were languishing. Their stock prices were near record lows and nobody wanted them. There was nothing fundamentally wrong with these companies; they just couldn't compete with the sexier, high-flying dot.coms. Where did the money go that fled the failing dot.coms? Surprisingly, some market analysts were recommending value stocks like Bank of America and General Motors.

Caution

When the Nasdaq passed 5,000, some people were saying the 10,000 mark would soon fall. Even after the index plunged 50 percent, some people were predicting it would hit 5,000 again and soon. All these predictions are idle speculation. No one knows where the index will be in six months.

The Nasdaq Composite Index dropped by 50 percent in one year as even the more established technology companies began reporting slowing growth and lower earnings. The market remains so fragile that a handful of technology companies can lead the Nasdaq up or drag it down. If Microsoft, one of the largest companies in the world, sneezes, the rest of the market gets pneumonia.

The market is notoriously fickle, and today's front-runner is tomorrow's also-ran. One way to reduce market risk is to avoid the current hot sector in favor of solid companies with long-term prospects. In retrospect, it's easy to see that many of the Internet wonders had no real chance for success in the long term. When the market becomes overheated for a particular sector, as it did for the Internet/technology stocks, you move out of the realm of investing and into a legalized form of gambling.

Tip

Speculating and investing are two different things. If you want to speculate in short-term trading, do so with the understanding that in the end you will lose more often than you will win.

A theory called the "Bigger Fool Theory" describes how a market reacts when it's overheated. In the past, it described oil and gas booms and real-estate runs. The Bigger Fool Theory states that it doesn't matter what you pay for the item because a bigger fool will come along and pay you more for it.

If you want to speculate in an overheated market, do it with money you can afford to lose. You should have a plan for entry and exit and stick with it. Be satisfied with merely obscene profits. Remember the golden rule of Wall Street: Bulls profit and bears profit, but pigs get slaughtered.

ECONOMIC RISK

Economic risk is when the economy turns against an investment. Perhaps interest rates go up or consumer demand goes down—either way your investment could be at risk.

For example, energy prices affect a wide range of industries; however, transportation companies and certain manufacturing concerns are particularly vulnerable. Automobile manufacturers and homebuilders suffer when interest rates rise sharply. A drop in consumer spending hurts discount stores and clothing manufacturers.

- **Recession.** Many of the preceding factors contribute to or manifest themselves during a recession, which usually leads to a bear market. The bear market of 1981–1983 was the result of then Fed Chairman Paul Volker raising interest rates to staggering heights. In Chapter 3, "Types of Bear Markets," we will look at inflation bear markets.

   When the Fed saw the economy contracting at a rate that indicated a recession was looming, it lowered interest rates in early 2001 in an attempt to head off the recession or at least soften the blow. Lowering interest rates is one way bear markets get back on their feet, although this alone isn't guaranteed to do the trick.

Plain English

Money supply is the cash circulating in the economy. The Fed controls the amount of cash and uses that control in its fight against inflation.

- **Fads and gimmicks.** Beware of companies built around fads and gimmicks. That may seem like overstating the obvious, but it's worth repeating. Someone will come out with a new doo-dad and, the next thing you know, it's all over the media. Companies that try to capitalize on these fads usually end up stuck with warehouses of product that no one wants.

- **Foreign threats.** Globalization is an economic reality, and although this process has many benefits, there are also some dangers. As economies become interdependent, the chances of a foreign crisis affecting U.S. markets increases. Political and economic unrest with key trading partners like Japan and Europe can affect U.S. markets.

- **Falling profits.** Another economic risk is falling profits from key industry leaders. There are usually a handful of leaders in every industry group. When these companies report stagnant or lower profits, the rest of the industry group also falter. If you don't own the leaders in a particular industry group, be aware your investments may suffer if the leaders don't meet earnings expectations.

T i p

The investing community watches earnings (profits) reports with great anticipation. When companies fail to make their earnings projections, the market batters the company's stock.

INFLATION RISK

One of the greatest economic risks to every sector of the economy is inflation. Inflation is when prices rise rapidly and the currency loses value. Simply stated, inflation is when too much money is chasing too few goods and services.

Inflation is the most feared of all economic maladies because it bleeds the value from investments and from workers' payroll checks. The Fed's primary job is to keep inflation under control. It uses interest rates and money supply to do this. If the Fed sees economic indicators pointing toward rising inflation, it will increase interest rates to cool off the economy. It did this six times during the last bull market.

Unfortunately, rising interest rates can have a chilling effect on the market and can ultimately lead to the bears taking over. Out-of-control inflation in the 1970s and 1980s contributed to numerous bear markets in this era. (See the table in Chapter 1, "Bear Markets.") It's a vicious cycle: The threat of returning inflation sets off interest-rate increases, which lead to a bear market and ultimately a recession. Lowering interest rates can break the bear market; however, this increases the threat of inflation.

C a u t i o n

Many economists consider inflation the most dangerous of economic problems. The Fed is willing to take extraordinary steps to keep it in check. Some of these steps, like rising interest rates, can hurt the stock market.

There is a delicate balance between stopping inflation and undoing a recession and bear market. Finding that balance is as much art as science.

WHERE TO HIDE

Investors traditionally look to hard assets like gold and real estate to protect themselves from the ravages of inflation. So-called hard assets have an intrinsic value that historically has done well in times of inflation—that is, until the 1980s, when gold, especially, took a beating.

Real-estate funds and inflation-indexed bonds are the most popular defenses against inflation today. I hope that the Fed will keep inflation under control. Those of us who lived through the hyperinflation of the 1970s and 1980s remember the pain and frustration of inflation.

INFLATION'S EVIL TWIN

Deflation is inflation's evil twin and is very rare. Deflation occurs when there are more goods and services than money. As with the stock market, when there are more sellers than buyers, the price drops. Deflation hurts companies by forcing them to reduce prices to stay competitive. This pressure can come from cheap foreign imports that flood the market.

Deflation hasn't happened on an economy-wide basis since the Great Depression. However, certain industries have suffered the effects of deflation in their particular market sectors. When inexpensive Japanese cars began pouring into the American economy, U.S. automakers reduced prices and introduced cheaper models to remain competitive.

U.S. industry has responded to the threat of cheap foreign competition by taking an "if you can't beat them, join them" strategy. Many manufacturers have moved all or parts of their operations overseas to take advantage of cheaper foreign labor. The threat of deflation is probably less because American-owned plants overseas make most of the cheap goods pouring into the U.S. market.

CONCLUSION

Investing is a contact sport. You can, and probably will, get hurt at some point. Whether it is a full bear market or a severe market correction, you need to be aware of the factors that lead to falling prices.

Information and education will help you structure your portfolio for the amount of protection you need at a particular point in your life.

Market risk, economic risk, and inflation risk are with you constantly, even if there is not a bear market in progress. In a bear market, these risks can become amplified and even more dangerous. You can't hope to achieve even modest returns without some risk. The trick is to keep the risk at a level you can tolerate and to be aware of the risk you have no control over.

CHAPTER 3

TYPES OF BEAR MARKETS

Knowing your enemy is half the battle. In a television commercial, basketball legend Bill Russell does a monologue about how he was so successful as a rebounder. He says that he knew every player's strengths and weaknesses; what they do in certain situations; what they are thinking before they shoot the ball. Russell concludes by saying he got most of his rebounds before the opponent even shot the ball.

Knowing your enemy is no less important in investing. Bear markets and market corrections can play havoc with your portfolio. Armed with information about how bear markets come about, you will be better prepared to deal with the consequences.

This chapter examines the different varieties of bear markets and how they affect your investments. In Part 3, "Bear Assets," we will look at these strategies in detail.

BEAR MARKET TYPES

In previous chapters, we looked at some of the causes of bear markets and some of the risks associated with investing in general. It is important to remember that often (maybe always) more than one factor causes bear markets. Sometimes a primary cause and contributing factors make the bear market particularly bad.

One chilling prospect is that we may be on the verge of seeing an entirely different type of bear market, one driven by large numbers of individual investors moving in concert thanks to the Internet.

In this chapter, we will look at the following types of bear markets, which I created for the purpose of explanation. These distinctions are arbitrary and there is not universal agreement about the causes of bear markets. It doesn't matter what you call them; the important thing is to see them coming.

- Political/financial-instability bear markets
- Market-liquidity bear markets
- Recession bear markets
- Inflation/interest-rate bear markets
- Deflation bear markets
- Information bear markets

Remember my caution from earlier: The closer you are to your financial goal (retirement, in particular), the more concerned you should be about bear markets and the more carefully you should watch the markets and the economy. A good financial advisor will help you watch for warning signs.

POLITICAL/FINANCIAL-INSTABILITY BEAR MARKETS

As economies of the world become more intertwined and dependent on each other, the potential for foreign instability to disrupt the stock market increases. The invasion of Kuwait in 1990 precipitated the bear market that set the stage for the 10-year bull market that ended with the 2000 disaster for Internet and tech stocks.

Wars and political instability are part of modern life. At any given time, there may be 30 to 40 wars in progress around the world. All wars are terrible, but the stock market is more concerned with some wars than others. The Gulf War that made Gen. Norman Schwarzkopf a hero was significant because instability in that part of the world threatened Middle Eastern oil supplies, which the United States depends heavily on to fuel our economy. Instability always leads to higher prices, and higher energy costs have a devastating effect on our economy; we could not allow those oil reserves to fall into unfriendly hands. The stock market is always looking forward: As the action in the Persian Gulf escalated, the stock market worried about the outcome and what it might mean for our economy. Would this be another Vietnam that would drag on for years and cost billions of dollars?

> **C a u t i o n**
>
> Energy prices are critical to our economy. Rising energy costs always have a negative affect on the economy and stock market.

Although we won the war, the stock market and economy suffered extensive damage. A bear market and a recession may have led to the defeat of President George Bush in the 1992 presidential election. The stock market's real concern with the Gulf War was the disruption of oil supplies from the region.

In Chapter 4, "Economic Indicators," we will look at some of the economic indicators that signal changes in the economy. When energy prices increase, you can be sure things are going to get worse, not better. As this is being written, California is experiencing rolling blackouts because of mismanagement by the state's utilities; crude oil is over $30 a barrel; and my natural gas bill is double what it was last year.

> **P l a i n   E n g l i s h**
>
> A **soft landing** is economist-speak for a recession that doesn't quite mature, but still has a negative affect on the economy.

The current debate is whether the economy will sink into a recession or have a "soft landing" with only short-term consequences. Even the experts don't know what will happen in the short run, but an unstable energy price scenario does not sound encouraging. Foreign oil problems are not the only threat to our financial well-being. A protracted recession in Japan and credit problems in Southeast Asia are sticky concerns for many U.S. companies looking to these areas for new markets. A severe recession with other major trading partners could have negative effects on our economy and the stock market.

MARKET-LIQUIDITY BEAR MARKETS

Market liquidity simply means there are plenty of buyers and sellers. When no one wants to buy a particular stock, you can bet the price will drop dramatically. Every market transaction requires two parties: the buyer and the seller. If one is absent or in short supply, the price will move in the opposite direction.

For example, John wants to sell his XYZ stock and hopes to get $50 per share. No one wants to buy XYZ. His options are to sit tight and hope buyers show up at $50 per share someday or to lower his price for the stock. However, even if he lowers his price, there is no guarantee he will find any buyers for his stock. On the other hand, if John wants to sell his stock for $50 per share, he might find several buyers for XYZ, and they bid the price up to $65 per share.

Tip ─────────────────────────────

> The most recent dramatic example of market liquidity occurred on Black Monday in October 1987, when the Dow Jones Industrial Average dropped over 500 points in one day. Sellers flooded the market; however, there were few buyers. The result was a huge drop in the market.

In the first scenario, there was no liquidity because John could not find any buyers for his shares. We assume that we can sell our stocks at any time. When there is a serious bear market, buyers will be hard to find. Stocks are not like bonds or certificates of deposit that have a fixed, and in the case of most CDs guaranteed, principle. Stocks are only worth what someone is willing to pay for them.

RECESSION BEAR MARKETS

Although it is sometimes difficult to separate the two, recessions and bear markets are not the same. It is possible (and it has happened) for there to be a bear market during good economic times and a bear market during a recession. It may be helpful to remember that the economy and the stock market are two faces of the same phenomenon. The difference is that the economy is looking backward to see how it did and the stock market is looking forward to see how it will do. These different perspectives account for why the economy may view one statistic as positive while the stock market may view the same statistic as negative.

I have used the example of unemployment figures before, but it's worth repeating. The economy views low unemployment figures as good because more people are working and contributing to the economy. For some companies, this may be a double-edged sword. It's good that consumers have more money to spend, but low unemployment means stronger competition for labor, which means high salaries and ultimately lower profits if the extra costs can't be passed on to customers. The company may lower future earnings estimates, which is sure to disappoint the market.

The intertwining of the economy and the stock market make them siblings, even though they may look in different directions. If the economy goes south, it can't be good for the market. A bear market spreads gloom and distrust, which erodes consumer confidence.

INFLATION/INTEREST-RATE BEAR MARKETS

The inflation/interest-rate bear market can be the most damaging to investors and the economy in general. The 1973–1974 bear market was especially devastating. (See the table in Chapter 1, "Bear Markets.") Economists believe that inflation is the most dangerous threat to our economy. The Fed's Chairman Alan Greenspan agrees. His best tool to fight inflation is interest rate adjustments. During the recent bull market, he raised interest rates six times in an attempt to cool off the white-hot economy. These interest rates, along with other factors, finally took hold in 2000 and the economy began to slow. Unfortunately, it looked like it was slowing too fast and headed for a recession. In an effort to prevent the recession or at least soften its blow, the Fed lowered interest rates in early 2000.

The falling stock market reacted predictably to the interest-rate hikes and slammed on the brakes. Higher interest rates mean money for expansion and growth is more expensive. Increased borrowing costs cut into future earnings. Investors began to worry about the double whammy of a bear market and a recession. The super hot Internet and technology stocks began to crumble in the spring of 2000. With a bear market and recession looming in the near future, investors dumped the former darlings of Wall Street for more secure issues.

As I noted earlier, one of the reasons the economy and the stock market don't always move in concert is they are influenced by the same factors, but from different perspectives.

Caution ────────────────────────────────

> Investors once assumed that there would always be "secure" issues to buy in times of turmoil. Don't assume past safe havens will remain so in the future.

LOOKING BACKWARD

The Fed must adjust interest rates based on information from the recent past, knowing that its actions may take some time to be effective. The stock market looks at information from the present and attempts to guess what impact it will have on future earnings and stock prices.

The stock market is so concerned about the future that it won't wait for official information. Investors anticipate the information before its release and act on it. The Fed normally meets on a quarterly basis and decides what to do about interest rates. The stock market makes an educated guess and moves before the meeting.

Tip ────────────────────────────────

> Analysts pore over every clue they can find to guess what the Fed will do to interest rates. Fed officials must be extremely cautious in public statements to not send unintended messages.

Normally, the market guesses right; but the Fed can surprise the market. When this happens, the market may react strongly. The Fed doesn't have to wait until its meeting to act. It can act whenever it feels the need. The stock market always greets these surprises with fevered activity.

WHAT DOES THIS MEAN TO YOU?

Investors are always looking to the future. You invest today in hopes of a gain in the future. You view the economy through this lens. Rising interest rates will almost certainly affect future earnings. Likewise, inflation will affect future earnings for most investments. Either rising interest rates or inflation can cause a bear market. The cure for inflation is raising interest rates. Either way, investors are stuck. In Chapter 4 we will look at indicators that you can watch for signs of rising interest rates and inflation along with other important indicators.

What you're looking for is a balance between a reasonable rate of inflation, economic growth, and interest rates. One could argue that such a balance facilitated the bull market and economic expansion of the 1990s. During this time, inflation averaged around 3 percent and interest rates, especially toward the end, were relatively low. The economy was growing at a rate that suggested inflation was a real possibility.

Caution

> A booming economy may not be great for the stock market. Rapid growth is a known cause of inflation, and the Fed watches growth numbers very carefully.

THE DEFLATION BEAR MARKET

Deflation, you'll remember, is the opposite of inflation. It occurs when prices fall dramatically because of outside factors such as the flood of cheap products into our markets. While it is unlikely we will face deflation anytime soon, the results would be devastating on the stock market. In the worst-case scenario, prices fall because of competitive pressure or some other factor. Corporate profits drop because costs don't fall along with prices. This squeezes profits, and investors flee to other investments.

A deflation bear market is more likely to occur in industry sectors than the total market. International trade agreements are constantly forged and revised to prevent this type of shock from foreign competitors.

INFORMATION BEAR MARKETS

History has much to tell us about bear markets. However, there have been dramatic changes in the stock markets and investors between the 1990 bear market and the current one. These changes might lay the groundwork for a new type of bear market I call the "information bear market." Admittedly, there is no scientific basis for this—and it hasn't happened yet. However, if you watch some of the cable financial news channels or visit many Web sites, you may notice how frantic they can make the market sound. This makes great drama but distorts reality by focusing on minute-to-minute market activity.

However, I think it's important to consider the changes not only in the technology of investing, but also the investors themselves.

THE TECHNOLOGY OF INVESTING

The process of investing in the stock market has changed dramatically during the last 25 years. What once was the exclusive purview of a handful of brokerage houses has become a wide-open market.

T i p

> When the market was roaring between 1998 and 2000, day traders attracted lots of media attention with their huge daily profits. After the bubble burst, they all but disappeared from the radar.

Younger investors may not remember that at one time you had to physically go to a stock brokerage to open an account to buy and sell stocks. The brokers fixed commissions at what would now seem criminally high rates. When these commissions were deregulated, a new type of stock brokerage emerged—the discount broker. The discount broker charged dramatically lower commissions, but investors received no research or help making investment decisions. Still, the lower commissions and the ease of dealing with the broker over the phone drew more investors into the stock market.

The next revolution occurred when the Internet gave birth to online stock brokerages. Their rates were even lower than discount brokers, and investors could do all their business online. Coupled with a booming economy and the hysteria associated with Internet/tech stocks, online investing exploded. Problems with broker Web sites crashing during heavy volume dulled some enthusiasm, but it didn't blunt the desire to trade.

With full-service brokers considered by many investors a thing of the past, investors who opted to trade with discount brokers (both on- and offline) had to do their own research, which is where the Internet really changed the playing field. Literally hundreds of Web sites offering information, research, and advice compete for investors' attention. You have access to more information today than at any time in history.

Caution

> Not all Web sites are equal. There are a number of great resources online, but there are also a number of thinly disguised sales pitches posing as "information."

The downside of this flood of information is the possibility that investors will panic or make hasty decisions based on information they receive in nearly real time. There have already been numerous cases of stock fraud by crooks using the Internet to spread false "news" about stocks in an attempt to manipulate the price. Admittedly, the big institutional investors and mutual funds are still the ones that dramatically affect the stock market, not individual investors.

There is no guarantee that individual investors won't panic as they did in the 1929 stock market crash. However unlikely this scenario is, you can't dismiss it.

CONCLUSION

Bear markets come in many flavors. Investors armed with information and education can prepare themselves in advance.

Interest rate increases in response to higher inflation is the cause of the most dangerous of all bear markets. Investors must prepare in advance for these problems because once they are upon the market, it may be too late.

CHAPTER 4

ECONOMIC
INDICATORS

Economics is known as the "dismal science." I'm not sure who gave it this label, but I suspect it was someone like me who's more comfortable with words than numbers. Unfortunately, you can't be very effective as an investor without getting familiar with the numbers.

Economic indicators are a selection of measurements used to understand the relative strength or weakness of the economy. Many of these numbers directly affect the stock market, so they are important to investors.

Most of these numbers are indexes, which means they represent the change from a base year. For example, the Employment Cost Index represents the change in the cost of labor. Economists use the numbers from 1989 as the base (1989 = 100). As labor costs change from quarter to quarter, the number relative to the base year changes. The number for the last quarter of 2000 was 150.6. However, the number most investors follow is the percent change. In this reporting period, that change was a 4.1 percent increase over the last quarter of 1999.

Plain English ───────────────────────────────

An **index** is a statistical composite that measures the increase or decrease of an economic indicator as measured against a base year.

We'll look at the Employment Cost Index in more detail later; however, economists report and measure many of the indicators we will look at in this section the same way. It's not particularly important that you understand how economists put the numbers together. (If you really want to know, many Internet sites and books report this information.) What *is* important is that you understand what these indicators mean in terms of your investments and understand how the stock market views them.

The market is always looking to the future. Rather than wait for the actual numbers, Wall Street economists make their own estimates of what the numbers will report. Investors, especially big institutional investors and mutual funds, make decisions based on these estimates. When the actual numbers differ substantially from estimates, the market will often react dramatically. A number of Web sites report the estimates and compare them to the actual numbers.

T i p

A number of Web sites, including TheStreet.com, publish a calendar of report dates for a variety of economic indicators. If you are interested in a particular indicator, the calendar will let you know when to look for the information.

Not every economic indicator has an important affect on the stock market, so we will stick with those that do.

INFLATION INDICATORS

As noted earlier, inflation is the most feared economic condition short of a depression. It robs value from just about every sector of the economy. Economists call inflation the evil tax because it takes value not only from your earnings but also from your principal. The Fed has demonstrated a willingness to go to great lengths to keep inflation in check. During the last leg of the recent bull market, the Fed raised interest rates six times in response to signs of impending inflation.

The following indicators represent the most important tools economists use to gauge the relative strength of inflation.

EMPLOYMENT COST INDEX

The Employment Cost Index (ECI) is an important measurement of inflation: It measures the change in the cost of employing workers and includes wages and employee benefits paid for by the employer. The Labor Department issues the report quarterly, and its change from the previous month and previous year is one of the best inflation barometers.

Economists attempt to predict the change from previous reports. Observers incorporate these expectations, along with other information and estimates, into market decisions. Analysts compare the actual numbers to the estimates. If there is a large difference, one way or the other, the market may react dramatically, since unexpected changes may affect the Fed's decisions regarding interest rates.

Let's look at the numbers reported for the last quarter of 2000 and see how this report may have affected the market. The Labor Department reported fourth-quarter numbers for 2000 on January 25, 2001. Economists estimated there would be a 1.1 percent increase in the fourth quarter from the third quarter. The actual increase was only 0.8 percent. When combined with a 0.9 percent increase from third quarter 2000, the numbers were a pleasant surprise for the market, showing that the ECI, or wage inflation, was slowing, and that it handily beat the estimate of 1.1 percent.

- Third quarter 2000: 0.9 percent
- Forecast fourth quarter 2000: 1.1 percent
- Actual fourth quarter 2000: 0.8 percent

This news justified the Fed's decision to lower interest rates, and further rate reductions may be possible. The market could feel good about the future of further rate reductions.

Of course, this is just one component of many that market economists consider along with the Fed in forecasting higher or lower inflation. Assuming no other indicators pointed in a different direction, you might consider investments that do well in an environment of lower or steady interest rates. Admittedly, long-term investors should probably not adjust their portfolios on just one quarter's information. However, a steady increase in the ECI suggests the Fed may raise interest rates.

The ECI began a fairly dramatic rise in the first quarter of 1999 and did not retreat until the fourth quarter of 2000. It isn't surprising that the Fed increased interest rates during this period.

PRODUCER PRICE INDEX

The Producer Price Index (PPI) reflects the prices received by producers. It includes the price of commodities at all stages of processing. The Labor Department issues the measure, with a base of 1982 = 100, monthly. There are two variations of the measure. The "core" measurement is the most important. It excludes highly volatile food and energy components, which can skew the results on a seasonal basis. The other measure includes these components but is considered unreliable because food and energy costs are so volatile.

Coupled with other inflation indicators, this number always affects the market. The PPI for December came out before the Employment Cost Index and was higher than expected, which created some concern that it might cause the Fed to keep its interest rate cut to one quarter of a point instead of the hoped-for one-half point reduction.

Caution

Economists forecast indicators to factor them into investment decisions before they happen. However, some indicators are so volatile that investors are reluctant to place too much value on estimates.

CONSUMER PRICE INDEX

The Consumer Price Index (CPI) may be more familiar to the public than some of the other indicators. The Labor Department releases the figures monthly. The index (1982–1984 = 100) reports the change in cost of a composite of such items as food, housing, energy, transportation, housing, clothing, education, entertainment, and healthcare. Like the PPI, the CPI "core" number excludes energy and food costs; economists believe the core number gives a clearer picture of inflation.

This is a significant measure of inflation and the stock market watches it closely. Market watchers consider the CPI a broader picture of inflation because it contains more components than the PPI, which does not include services.

The December 2000 number, reported in mid-January 2001, came in just where the economists estimated, with the core number slightly under estimates. This was good news for the market because it confirmed that inflation was under control.

Now we have three numbers for inflation during the month of January 2001. The Fed's regularly scheduled meeting at the end of the month would consider interest rates. What would they do? A CPI moving up over several months is a cause for concern. The Fed is likely to either raise interest rates or leave them the same. In a bear market, raising interest rates to combat inflation would prolong the bear's visit. Good news on the inflation front likely means lower interest rates, which are good for stocks and bonds.

Tip

> The Fed funds rate is a base rate that banks use when they lend to each other overnight. It is the short-term rate upon which other rates (mortgages, consumer loans, and so on) are set.

It would seem that the indicators favored a controlled inflation. If these were the only numbers used by the Fed, it would be safe to assume that interest rates won't be going up soon.

MORE ECONOMIC INDICATORS

Economists follow many other economic indicators, and those that follow can have a significant influence on the stock market. Even though I have not included them under the inflation indicators, many would fit.

EMPLOYMENT REPORT

The Employment Report is one of the best measures of the economy's health. There are actually four numbers: the unemployment rate, new jobs created, length of workweek, and average hourly wages. The Labor Department issues this report monthly, and market observers watch it with anticipation.

Changes in these numbers can move the market dramatically. Strong numbers in these reports indicate a growing and healthy economy, which is a good thing. However, if the economy appears to be growing too fast, it can lead to inflation.

T i p

> The unemployment rate stayed at record low levels for much of the latter 1990s. As the economy began to slow, the rate began to creep upward.

A healthy economy has a low unemployment rate, creates new jobs, increases the workweek, and raises hourly wages. An economy growing too fast in these categories creates inflation. On the other hand, a slowing economy has rising unemployment, fewer new jobs created, short workweeks, and falling hourly wages. The stock market may not view numbers that look good for the economy in a positive manner. Low unemployment is a sign of a healthy economy; however, it can mean higher labor costs for employers, which can cut into profits.

The Fed must do an incredible balancing act between keeping inflation under control and keeping the economy moving at a positive pace. Raising interest rates to slow inflation may have the effect of slamming the brakes on the economy. The Employment Report is critical to their deliberations. The stock market wants lower interest rates, but not at the expense of inflation.

C a u t i o n

> Changing the direction of the economy is like steering a large ship; it usually takes some time before any changes are apparent.

The fear in the stock market as 2000 became 2001 was that the economy was decelerating too rapidly. A bear gripped the stock market and investors were afraid a recession would only make things worse. Inflation was clearly in check, so the Fed cut interest rates twice in January 2001 for a 1 percent decrease. However, even this was not enough to lift the market and economy in a substantial way—at least not yet. Interest rate moves take some time to filter through the economy. It may be several months after a change in interest rates before the effect spreads throughout the economy.

It is important to remember that bad numbers in the Employment Report can lead to higher or static interest rates. The market may react swiftly to an interest rate decision, but it will take some time for the rate changes to affect earnings.

PURCHASING MANAGERS' INDEX

The Purchasing Managers' Index (PMI) is the most important indicator of the manufacturing sector. The National Association of Purchasing Management produces the PMI and reports their findings at the first of each month. They survey some 300 purchasing managers from manufacturing companies for the index. The PMI numbers are different from the other indexes we have discussed: The index is neutral at 50; any number over 50 is a sign of expansion, and any number under 50 is a sign of contraction.

There are a number of components to the PMI, but your concern is with the expansion or contraction of the manufacturing sector. The PMI gives you a good picture of the economy on a month-to-month basis. Scores above 50 indicate the economy is growing; however, a strong number above 50 may signal an overheated economy. Along with the Durable Goods Orders Report, the PMI is a major barometer of the economy's health.

A look at the 2000 PMI numbers shows an almost unbroken string of declining numbers. The December 2000 number of 43.7 was far below estimates and sent a strong signal that the economy was stalling faster than expected—this was the lowest score since 1991. The run continued in January 2001 with a 41.2 PMI. This 13-month decline signals a slowing economy, and the corresponding bear market confirms the strong tie between manufacturing and the stock market.

DURABLE GOODS ORDERS

The Durable Goods Orders Report tracks orders received by manufacturers of products designed to last three years or more. "Durable goods" include automobiles, factory machinery, airplanes, consumer appliances, and so on. The Census Bureau reports this number monthly.

This is an important economic indicator for the manufacturing component of the economy. Although not a large component of our economy, its health is of major importance, and soft or declining numbers in this report signal a weakening economy. Fewer orders for durable goods means companies that provide supplies to manufacturers will see reduced demand for their products and services; workers along the supply chain are no longer working overtime—and may lose their jobs; workers facing uncertain earnings cut back on spending to preserve cash; and so on. It's not uncommon for the Employment Report and the Durable Goods Orders Report to move together.

Caution

> A slowdown in manufacturing can ripple through the whole economy. Whole towns have suffered terribly when factories closed because of the wages—and expendable income—those workers have lost.

The Durable Goods Orders Report is highly volatile. Many observers back out the transportation component, which can skew the results. For example, the December 2000 report showed a 2.2 percent increase in new durable goods orders over November 2000. This surprised analysts who expected a 1.7 percent decrease for the period. When observers adjusted the report for a large commercial aircraft order, it showed that new durable goods orders actually fell 1.4 percent.

These reports gave the Fed freedom to reduce interest rates further, which they did at the end of January 2001. Market observers noted that by mid-February 2001, Fed Chairman Alan Greenspan gave a speech warning of a rapidly slowing economy. This led some to believe the Fed may be considering further interest rate cuts. As noted earlier, interest rate changes may have an immediate affect on the stock market, but they may not offset a slowing economy, which suggests lower earnings and lower stock prices.

Caution

> Interest rates grease the wheels of the economy, but rate adjustments aren't a "silver bullet" that solve all economic problems.

INDUSTRIAL PRODUCTION AND CAPACITY UTILIZATION

The Industrial Production and Capacity Utilization Report adds the third leg to the important manufacturing sector reports, measuring changes in production at factories and analyzing the capacity and utilization of our factories, mines, and utilities. The Federal Reserve issues the report monthly.

The percent change from month to month paints a picture of where the manufacturing sector is heading, and the December 2000 number shows a decline of 0.6 percent. The Federal Reserve also reported that industrial output contracted at a 1.1 percent annualized rate. Like the PMI number, this was the first contraction since 1991.

The information for December 2000 I used to illustrate the three manufacturing measures reveals a consistent and troubling picture: All three reports suggest a dramatic slowing of the economy and build a strong case for further intervention by the Fed on interest rates. Hard numbers like these make it easier to understand why corporate earnings are suffering and stock prices are in a bear's grip.

Caution

You can always find market commentators on the Internet and elsewhere who want to paint a picture of the economy to suit their own particular prejudices. Unfortunately, numbers are stronger than words. You can't wish away bad news.

RETAIL SALES

The Retail Sales Report totals sales at retail stores, but it does not include services. The Census Bureau issues this report monthly, usually within two weeks of the previous month's end.

Consumer spending is a strong force in our economy, so market observers closely watch this report, which has significance for the market in the short-term and contributes to the larger picture of economic health. Strong retail sales signal a healthy economy. Slowing retail sales may indicate consumers are contemplating tighter times ahead and are putting off nonessential spending. (You would expect to see low unemployment correlate with a good retail sales report.) A dramatic slowing of retail sales can hasten an economic slowdown and a strong increase in retail sales can help pull the economy out of a downturn.

The December 2000 Retail Sales Report showed a small 0.1 percent increase. The two previous reports showed declines, combining for a shaky prognosis for 2001. This fits into the picture we have drawn using December 2000 numbers for the major economic indicators.

GROSS DOMESTIC PRODUCT

The Gross Domestic Product (GDP) is the measure of how fast the economy is growing or shrinking. The Commerce Department issues the report on the change in the price of all goods and services produced by the economy on a quarterly basis. The *advance report* is first; the *preliminary* is the revision of the first estimate; and the *second revision* is the final report. There is about one month between each report.

The GDP is an important piece of the economic indicator puzzle. Market analysts closely watch the GDP since it represents how fast the economy is growing, which relates directly to the stock market. If the actual GDP numbers differ significantly from estimates, the market may react strongly. The GDP is widely reported in the media, although they seldom give you enough information to understand whether it is good news or not.

Continuing our look at economic indicators reported in January 2001, we find the GDP released on the last day of the month for the fourth quarter of 2000 showed the economy growing by only 1.4 percent. Market watchers had forecast a 1.9 percent increase and were surprised at how much the economy was contracting. The 1.4 percent growth was the lowest since 1995.

C a u t i o n

> Investors expect companies to keep growing and increasing the value of their investment. During slowing economies, many companies have trouble maintaining growth rates. This can spell trouble if the company has spent heavily building an infrastructure to support growth. If growth slows, the revenues to pay for the infrastructure may drop and cause profits to suffer.

A slowing economy, as represented by the economic indicators above, spells trouble for corporations that need to maintain a growth rate or raise their earnings. On the other hand, a GDP that is rising too fast can indicate an economy that may produce inflation. Either way, the GDP is important to watch.

CONCLUSION

Is your head swimming? This was probably a lot more about economic indicators than you wanted to know, but the relationship between the economy and the stock market is important to your investment decisions. Understanding what's happening in the economy can suggest sound investment strategies.

CHAPTER 5

MARKET INDICATORS

You would think with all the economic indicators we just plowed through in Chapter 4 and all the numbers that spew forth from the Internet, that only an idiot couldn't see a bear market coming.

But if it were that easy, you wouldn't need this book! Unfortunately, bears are hard to spot. Sometimes they come in the front door, and sometimes the back. We have also learned in earlier chapters that certain influences completely outside the market, such as war, can invoke a bear. Nevertheless, it's important to keep an eye on market indicators for warning signs. The stock market gives off all kinds of signs; interpreting which ones are real bears and which are bear traps is as much an art as a science. The prudent investor hopes for the best and prepares for the worst.

In this chapter, we will look at some of the market indicators that can help us spot a bear market. We'll look at some of the more common indicators as well as some that aren't so well known. Like the economic indicators from the previous chapter, no single sign clearly foretells an approaching bear. Like pieces of a puzzle, these indicators construct a picture that previously was a jumble of random signs.

Tip

> Warning signs are of no importance if you are not prepared to act. Every investor should have a plan for every asset you own, whether it is an individual stock or a mutual fund.

MAJOR MARKET INDEXES

The "roaring '90s" drew a tremendous amount of media attention to the stock market, which drew a number of new investors. Dazzling reports of dot.com billionaires and day traders dominated the news. "The Dow," "the S&P 500," and "the Nasdaq" became household words as they set one record after another.

Let's look beyond the numbers to see what these and other major market indexes can tell us. There is no way to accurately predict the future direction of these indexes, and even though individual stocks do not necessarily follow major indexes, the reality is that many do. Understanding what part of the market they represent is helpful in getting a sense of what the future holds for your investments, and helps you understand why one index is rising while another is falling.

Caution

> You can buy futures contracts on most of the major indexes. Some investors use these to protect themselves against market swings. Futures contracts, options, and other derivatives are valid investment tools, but only in the hands of the most experienced investors.

Watching indexes can lead to a short-term mindset. Investors are still digesting the emergence of more than one "market." Although this situation has been around for some time, the recent skyrocketing and subsequent crash of the Nasdaq has focused more attention on understanding the differences between multiple markets.

In many ways, you get a clearer picture of what is happening from the economic indicators we discussed in the last chapter. Nevertheless, what follows is a quick overview of the major indexes and some sense of how they fit into the overall picture. Some of the tools listed below will help you understand what the market is doing over time, and more tools are available if you're interested in pursuing technical analysis further.

THE DOW JONES INDUSTRIAL AVERAGE

The Dow Jones Industrial Average is the oldest and most widely reported of the major market indexes. If a news outlet reports only one indicator, it will be the Dow. When people speak of the broad market, they are often referring to the Dow.

The Dow covers just 30 stocks. You may find it difficult to accept that 30 stocks can represent "the broad market." However, these stocks are all leaders in their respective industries. As a broad generalization, sectors tend to follow their leaders. When you hear the term "blue-chip stock," think of the Dow. Leaders lead, and if you own stocks or mutual funds, watching the Dow is an important part of your work.

Plain English

A **"blue-chip" stock** is a premium investment. These are well-established and respected companies with lengthy histories of good returns. The term "blue chip" comes from poker, where the blue chips are worth the most.

The Dow also plays an important role in registering the "mood" of the market. You cannot take emotion out of any market observation; the market (Dow) reflects the optimism or pessimism of the investing community. A 20 percent decline in the Dow over a sustained period qualifies as a bear market.

THE NEW YORK STOCK EXCHANGE COMPOSITE INDEX

The New York Stock Exchange (NYSE) Composite Index covers all the stocks traded on the exchange. Although not as widely quoted as the Dow, it is a good indicator of how larger companies are doing.

Obviously, its coverage of a large number of stocks gives it greater claim to representing "the broad market." The NYSE stocks tend to be older, more established companies. The listing qualifications exclude smaller companies. Small, startup companies led the late-1990s bull market. For this reason, the NYSE probably didn't represent the heart of the bull market.

This index will track the Dow, although its broader coverage reduces some of its volatility. This makes the NYSE a widely used proxy for "the market." It takes more than a few bad reports on individual stocks to move the NYSE index.

STANDARD & POOR'S 500

Standard & Poor's 500 (S&P 500) is the most widely used index by investing professionals. It represents 500 of the largest companies, and many believe it is the best "broad market" indicator. Investment professionals, particularly mutual fund managers, compare their performance to the S&P 500.

Its broader coverage makes it more accurate than the Dow, and because of its focused approach to selecting components, it is more representative than the NYSE Composite Index.

Tip ───────────────────────────────

> Mutual-funds managers in particular use the S&P 500 as a benchmark for their funds performance. When they beat the S&P 500, managers proudly display the fact in the annual report. If they don't beat the mark, look for many excuses.

The relative health of "the market" is of little consequence if your investments tank. The S&P 500 is a measure of where the mainstream market is at any one time. The prudent investor should find most of their investments in or close to "the market." Fringe investments usually are the first casualties of a downturn.

THE NASDAQ COMPOSITE INDEX

The Nasdaq Composite Index covers the 5,000-plus companies in the Nasdaq market. These companies are, for the most part, smaller than their counterparts on the NYSE. (Nasdaq originally was NASDAQ, which stood for National Association of Securities Dealers Automated Quotations. It has since evolved into a complete stock market and is now simply the Nasdaq National Market.) However, Microsoft, the off-and-on largest company in the world, is on the Nasdaq.

That's the appeal of investing in smaller companies. One day they may grow up to be the next Microsoft. The Nasdaq is where the dot.com boom flourished in the late 1990s. Companies went from an idea to market caps in the tens of billions of dollars, seemingly overnight.

This makes the Nasdaq highly volatile, because those small companies can go from boom to bust to boom in the blink of an eye and because a handful of Microsoft-like companies can drive the index in either direction. The Nasdaq topped 5,000 and, then in less than a year, lost almost 50 percent of its value. If one of the tech leaders falters, you can be sure the Nasdaq will not react well. For this reason, the Nasdaq is not a reliable short-term indicator of the general market.

C a u t i o n

> What goes up must come down. That may not always be true; however, when a market overheats as the Nasdaq did in the final years of the last bull market, a severe bear is almost inevitable.

WHAT DO MARKET INDICATORS TELL US ABOUT BEARS?

As I noted earlier, bear markets seldom follow a direct line of declining market numbers. They are often marked with ups and downs that sometimes are simply corrections. Market observers watch the movement and look for lower lows and lower highs as signs of market momentum moving from bull to bear.

These observations should cover several days to avoid bear traps of sharp declines followed by rebounds. Lower lows and lower highs mark a definite and visible trend. The opposite would be true when the market moves out of a bear and into a bull frame of mind. There will be higher highs and higher lows.

VOLUME SIGNS

Watching the market volume (the number of shares traded) can give you additional confirmation as to the "lower lows and lower highs" approach. As the market hits these marks, take note if volume is increasing or decreasing. If volume is increasing from one lower low to the next (within a couple of days), you may be looking at a bear. What you are seeing is downward momentum, and it can be a powerful force in the market.

Unsupported lows may be a bear trap. On the other hand, when the market hits new lower lows and lower highs on increasing volume, you are looking at a dangerous trend downward.

The opposite works for emerging bull markets. Higher highs and higher lows mark the way out of a bear market if volume is increasing along the way.

Tip

Rising volume indicates more people and more issues are participating in the market. This positive signal reflects the fact that once the market moves strongly in one direction, it takes extreme measures to reverse its course.

Volume of shares traded is a good indication of the market's feeling about the short-term future. It is important to remember that the market is always thinking ahead. When investors note the market indexes rising on ever-increasing volume, it is a sign of optimism. The market is saying things are going to get better. However, the opposite is also true. When volume rises on a declining market, investors are saying they're concerned about the short-term future.

ADVANCE-DECLINE SIGNS

The advance-decline line is another tool that investors use to gain some sense of where the market's heading. The A/D line is a way to measure the market's breadth: a graphical representation of the market's strength of movement relative to the number of stocks advancing and the number declining.

The calculation is to take the number of issues advancing minus the number of issues declining. Add the result to a cumulative total for plotting. When more stocks are declining than advancing, the line heads downward; when there are more advances than declines, the line rises. (The number isn't important—we're just looking for a direction.) At a glance, investors can see which way the market is headed, how long it has been moving that way, and so on. The A/D line may be more accurate for identifying market strength than the indicators we've already discussed, and you can use it with any major index. (StockChart.com is a great place to build these charts with relative ease.)

The A/D line can also point out anomalies in the market. This occurs when the A/D line for a major index is headed one way and the index is headed another. The following illustration from Equis.com shows the A/D line for the Dow leading up to the 1987 disaster. The A/D line is heading downward while the Dow is still trying to hit new highs.

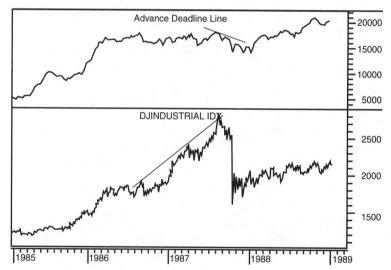

The A/D line and Dow going opposite ways.

When the A/D line and the index are moving in opposite directions, it's called a divergence. Divergences usually indicate a change. The index usually follows the A/D line. Looking at this chart would send chills down the back of investors who followed the A/D charts.

The problem with following the A/D line is that it doesn't look forward. You can't know what it is going to look like next week by looking at it this week.

Several other indicators are built around the advancing and declining issues, including one that measures not the number of issues but the volume. Market watchers calculate the volume of advancing issues and the volume of declining issues and chart this line. I suggest you visit Equis (www.equis.com) for more information on these indicators and how you can use them.

TECHNICAL ANALYSIS OF THE MARKETS

Many investors rely on technical analysis to tell them about the health of the market. Technical analysis attempts to predict the movement of the market using volume, prices, new highs and lows, and other market data. Investors using technical analysis rely on charts to display trends of issues like momentum, volume, and other information that gives them a clue about market direction.

Investors use technical analysis as a way to predict price movement of individual stocks. The adherents use charts to watch a stock's movement, looking for buy or sell signs. Technical analysts pore over charts with the zeal of an explorer looking for the "X" that "marks the spot."

Technical analysis has much to offer, but it's not the final answer; it's just another tool for examining a complicated picture. It's not particularly good at predicting long-term trends, so most investors find that combining elements of technical analysis with other observations makes more sense than relying on just one tool.

A comprehensive look at technical analysis is beyond the scope of this book, so we've just touched on a few popular tools. There are a number of resources at the end of this book that you can use for more information.

EARNINGS FORECASTS

Investors are concerned primarily with the future. One of the strongest positive signs for investors is a market leader reporting positive earnings estimates. This is welcome news to investors even if they don't own those individual stocks; good news in the earnings estimate report means companies are optimistic about the near-term health of their company.

One company reporting bad earnings estimates may not move the market, but when other market leaders start warning that they may not hit earlier estimates or release new estimates that show a decline in earnings, the market takes notice.

Tip

When companies begin making or revising earnings estimates lower than the market anticipated, you can bet the stock will fall. If several stocks that are leaders drop, the whole market may retreat.

The other number investors watch closely is growth in sales, especially for young companies that may not be profitable yet. Growth estimates reflect health in the company's market; declining growth signals trouble ahead.

Neither earnings estimates nor future growth are widely reported in the aggregate for the market. However, when talk in the media is of declining earnings estimates or growth figures, the future is cloudy at best.

WHAT DO BOND INVESTORS TELL US?

Bonds, like stocks, are bets on the future. Although they differ in many ways, both stocks and bonds hope to capitalize on the future.

If you buy a newly issued 10-year Treasury bond, you expect to earn a higher interest rate than if you bought a 1-year Treasury bond. The reason is that bonds are very interest-rate sensitive: As interest rates go up, bond prices go down. For example, if your 10-year bond had an interest rate of 8 percent and open interest rates went to 9 percent, you would have to discount the price of the bond to sell it.

However, as interest rates go down, bond prices go up. Your 10-year bond with an 8 percent interest rate would command a premium when market interest rates drop to 6 percent.

Tip

> Bonds may do well in a bear market if the Fed is dropping interest rates to soften the landing.

Bond yields reflect the current price of the bond and its coupon interest rate. You would expect long-term bonds to have a higher yield than a short-term bond. (Long-term bonds are at a higher risk from inflation and other economic problems than short-term bonds.) When the yield of short-term bonds exceeds those of long-term bonds, a recession and bear market are definite possibilities. This "inverted" yield curve expresses pessimism about the future.

CONCLUSION

This brief introduction to market indicators is meant to show you that investors need to keep their eyes open to changing conditions. As you'll see in later chapters, this will help you prepare for bear markets or severe corrections.

No set of magic indicators will tell you what the market will look like next month, much less next year, but you can lower the odds that a bear will blindside you at the worst possible time—when you're unprepared.

PART 2

BEAR TRAPS

I'm a big advocate of the "buy low, sell high" theory of investing. It has been my experience that you can make money doing this. Unfortunately, the theory has one small problem: It doesn't always work. It doesn't work because it relies on correctly buying at the bottom and selling at the top, and no one can call the turns with consistent accuracy.

Investors, even professionals, find market timing too tempting to resist at times. On the other hand, it takes nerves of steel to sit on your "buy-and-hold" strategy while watching your investments sink like a brick in an extended bear market.

Sometimes bad things happen to good investments, but, most often, bad things happen to bad investments. Either way, you need an exit plan when you see a bear market coming or when you find yourself in the middle of an unstable market that is throwing off confusing signals.

You need a plan to deal with falling prices before they start falling. This part of the book looks at market timing and how to avoid this particularly nasty bear trap. We will also spend some time on developing a strategy for selling a stock and a mutual fund. The strategies for selling stocks and mutual funds differ in some respects because of the difference in the two investments, but there are also many similarities.

CHAPTER 6

MARKET TIMING: THE TWO MOST DANGEROUS WORDS IN INVESTING

Two hikers are on their way up a mountain trail when a large bear spots them and charges. One hiker immediately drops to the ground, pulls her running shoes out of the backpack, and begins taking off her hiking boots.

"Are you crazy?" her companion shouts. "You can't outrun a bear!"

She looks up at him and says, "I don't have to outrun the bear. I just have to outrun you."

You can't outrun a bear market either. It's tempting to *think* you can, by timing your entry and exit in an unstable market, but the overwhelming evidence is that market timing doesn't work consistently, and leaving may be more harmful than doing nothing.

There are two forms of market timing: intentional and unintentional. Both are deadly to your portfolio.   ·

INTENTIONAL MARKET TIMING

It seems so simple. Buy when stock prices are low and sell when they are high. Thousands of investors are unable to resist the temptation: All they need do is look back at the stock that went from $10 per share to $50 per share to see how easy this is.

Unfortunately, 20/20 hindsight doesn't help you look forward. It doesn't help you identify the stock that went from $10 to $50 any more than it warns you about the stock that went from $50 to $10.

MARKET TIMERS

Market timing has its proponents. You don't have to look very far or hard to find folks who will gladly call the market turns for you if you subscribe to their service. Some of these market timers are very sincere about their approach and believe they can provide a real service.

Others, however, are just short of frauds. One of their tools is trotting out "historical" data that shows how their system called the market correctly for the past 10 years, or whatever. They base many of their systems on back testing, which takes a trading system and applies it against historical market data. Done objectively, there is nothing wrong with this approach. However, if you manipulate the system to produce the best results based on the historical data, you have crossed the line between testing and moved into the realm of shell games: You can't duplicate their results because they tweaked the system to work with a market that won't exist again.

C a u t i o n

> Save your money and don't invest in expensive newsletters that offer to predict market turns. There is no credible evidence that they work.

The sincere proponents of market timing don't promise triple-digit returns every year. Instead, they hope to improve your odds by suggesting possible market turns based on fundamental and technical analysis.

Most market timers appear to be do-it-yourselfers. A striking example of this band of hardy souls is the day trader. You remember day traders don't you? In the waning years of the 1990s, they were the hottest act on

Wall Street. You couldn't open an investing publication or cruise the Internet without reading about a former cab driver making $50,000 a week day trading at his kitchen table in his underwear. When the dot.coms became dot.bombs, the day traders disappeared from the media. The untold story, even during their peak, was that very few day traders were making money even when the market was red-hot.

Another form of market timing that ran rampant during this period was the IPO craze. Just about any new Internet or tech company that went public experienced huge run-ups of its stock almost overnight. This was the origin of the dot.com billionaires who became so famous. Most of their wealth was in the stock and stock options they held. Investors tried to cash in on the huge gains, and some managed to do so by buying early and getting out quickly with a reasonable profit, but the market wasn't very kind to those who got in late and didn't get out quickly. The super-high prices for most of these stocks didn't hold, and people lost much of their investment.

Caution ───

> The IPO craze drove people to pay incredible prices for young companies with no track record. In fact, many of the companies had no profits and no working products.

For example, I am aware of a company that went public around $20 per share. Within a short period, the stock was selling for over $100 per share. It didn't stay there long and fell to $14 per share. All of this happened in less than 12 months. (As I write this, the stock is trading for $23 per share less than two years after it went public.)

The sad truth is that many of the hot IPOs were trading at or below their offering price within six months to one year. After the Nasdaq meltdown that began in the spring of 2000, many of these former high-flyers have disappeared altogether.

THE UNINTENTIONAL MARKET TIMER

The unintentional market timer is the investor who jumps into the market without much of a plan and has no idea what to do when things turn sour. People are very emotional about their money—especially when they're losing it. They jump in impulsively and bail out without much more consideration.

The late-1990s bull market made making money look so easy, and attracted many investors with little or no experience in the market. Investors and potential investors watched the Internet/tech stocks go crazy along with the Nasdaq index. Typically, they waited until the market was way up before investing; then, deciding the bull market was going to be around for a while, they charged into the market. With no real knowledge of market dynamics, they bought overpriced stocks that ultimately proved to have only one way to go with any momentum—and that was down.

When the market turned and their stocks began to fall, they watch helplessly as their money evaporated. Some cut their losses quickly or even took a small profit. Others froze like deer in the headlights. Perhaps they convinced themselves that a "buy and hold" strategy would see them through. When prices didn't bounce back, they sold in frustration and left the market in disgust. But not just the novices suffered. A number of seasoned professionals also took big hits because they put aside their disciplined approach to investing and ran with the excitement.

Caution

> The heady days of the Internet/tech bull market were full of optimism and a sense that anyone could make a fortune in the market. Unfortunately, when the bubble broke, many watched the market fall, sure it would bounce back any minute. Markets do fall, and they can fall much farther than you think.

THE TRUTH ABOUT MARKET TIMING

The truth is that market timing, intentional or otherwise, doesn't work. No one can consistently call market turns and neither can you. (I can't either.) Here are some simple truths about market timing:

- No one knows what the market will do tomorrow, next week, or next year.
- Unless index funds make up your portfolio, there is no guarantee that your investments will turn with the market.

* In most cases, you are probably better off invested than not: Buy and hold.
* Timing the market takes a lot of time.
* Timing the market often builds huge tax bills.

NO ONE KNOWS THE MARKET

No matter how many numbers you crunch, there is no way to figure out what the market is going to do next with any degree of accuracy. For all the numbers and analysis, stock prices are still reflections of expectations. If investors expect a company to be more profitable in six months, today's price reflects that expectation. But a lot can happen in six months. Active investors (those who trade often) even have another layer of expectations: What stock will everyone else want in six months?

Add in unanticipated factors outside the market, and you can see why knowing the market's next move is so complicated.

Tip

It is hard not to be impressed with some of the Internet pundits writing and making predictions about the market, but if you check the site archives, you may find that their track record is not so great.

Anyone who tells you what the market is going to do next month is guessing. When you guess, sometimes you are right, and sometimes you are wrong.

YOUR INVESTMENTS MAY NOT FOLLOW THE MARKET

Although the majority of stocks will follow a bear market to lower prices, it is not true of every stock or even every stock sector. Historically, utilities and dividend-rich stocks have done better in slowing markets than other sectors. Food and consumer staples tend to hold up well in bear markets. (People still need to eat and brush their teeth.)

You can't be sure that your investments are going to drop at the same rate as the market. Some (such as technology stocks) may drop considerably faster and farther than other sectors.

Some advisors suggest that you put your money in a good stock index fund and forget about it. An S&P 500 index fund is going to rise and fall with the market. If you have a long time horizon before you need your money, this is an easy way to ride out down markets. That is not always the best strategy, however, especially if you're approaching a financial goal such as retirement.

YOU'RE BETTER OFF INVESTED

There is significant evidence that staying invested in common stocks or stock funds is a good defense against a bear market. Investors who suffered through the super bear market in 1973 and 1974 were sorely tested. It must have been difficult to watch the market bleed out almost 50 percent of its value.

The investment community has a lot of respect for the "buy-and-hold" strategy. Unfortunately, investors don't always listen to the *full* strategy; they assume that if they buy a stock they should hold it forever. Simply put, if you buy a piece of junk today, it will still be a piece of junk in 10 years. "Buy and hold" assumes you acquire quality investments and they remain quality investments during the holding period.

In Chapters 7 and 8, we will discuss when it is time to sell a stock or a mutual fund. As I said earlier, bad things happen to good stocks. When they do, you need a plan and methodology for deciding when to sell.

The buy-and-hold strategy also assumes you have a long-time horizon before you need these investments for a financial goal. As we saw in Chapter 1, it can take years to recover from a bear market. If you are looking at retirement in a few years, you cannot afford to wait through a lengthy bear market and lengthy recovery. Unfortunately, your options are more limited if a bear catches you unprepared. In Chapters 8 and 9, we discuss preparing your portfolio for retirement by moving assets into more secure investments.

What can you do? First, don't panic. Now is the time for some very careful decisions. Too many investors react in an emotional manner and take themselves out of the market. You cannot afford to abandon the market completely. Remember, you may have 20-plus years of retirement to support. The market has historically returned close to 12 percent, and you will need some significant returns to make your remaining assets stretch.

Don't make the gambler's mistake of "doubling up to catch up." In other words, high-risk investments may have gotten you into this mess, but they won't get you out. Consider moving into lower-risk products like bonds, real estate investment trusts, and income-producing (dividend) stocks.

The hardest decision of all may be to go back to work or not retire immediately. Delaying retirement or going back to work will give you much-needed cash and give your investments a chance to recover. The longer you delay withdrawals from your investments, the longer they will earn a return for you.

You will do yourself a big favor by contacting an investment professional to review your situation before making any big steps. The right course of action depends on the assets you're holding and many other factors unique to each investor. Make this move quickly to minimize the damage.

TIMING THE MARKET TAKES TIME

If you feel you just have to try market timing, be prepared to spend most of your time staring at your computer screen. You need patience and practice to find the perfect moment to trade. Ask any day trader how much time they spend watching for those moments. In the end, you will still be wrong more times than you are right.

A number of software packages and online services will help you spot trading times. Most of the tools used by market timers involve technical analysis: studying price movement and volume numbers of individual stocks. The goal is to find a moment when a stock's high is not going to hold or when the stock has hit bottom and is on the way up. Technical analysts plot the numbers on charts and analyze them for patterns. A number of Internet sites construct and update charts on selected stocks.

> **Tip**
>
> Technical analysis is an important tool in deciding when to buy and sell an investment; however, you should use it in connection with a fundamental analysis of the investment for maximum effectiveness.

I believe technical analysis can provide valuable information to investors, but it's not a science with foolproof results. Purists trade stocks of companies they know nothing about other than that the charts look good. This seems to violate one of the important rules of investing: *Know what you are buying.*

YOU HAVE TO PAY THE TAX MAN

I have an agreement with my tax-attorney friends that I repeat in all my books: I don't practice tax law, and they don't sue me. So far, it's working out pretty well.

Active investors, folks that trade frequently, are almost by definition market timers. They are looking for an opportunity to jump in, take a profit, and retreat. They may not trade as often as day traders, but they trade much more frequently than the average investor. These frequent trades can create a hefty tax bill.

Investments held less than one year are subject to tax just like regular income. You will need to pay any federal, state, or local taxes; Social Security and Medicare taxes; and any other applicable tax. Factor in brokers' fees and any services you pay for, and it becomes clear you need to be very good at market timing to keep your head above water.

AVOIDING SNAP DECISIONS

As I noted earlier in this chapter, the unintentional market timer is prone to making snap decisions on when to enter the market and when to exit. These decisions are usually wrong, and if they aren't wrong, you just got lucky.

There is no substitute for doing your homework before you buy a stock or mutual fund. There are numerous books (including *Alpha Teach Yourself Investing in 24 Hours,* Alpha Books, 2000) that will give you the tools and information you need for successful investing.

Equally important but often overlooked is a notion of how and under what circumstances you will sell the investment. We will cover that topic in detail in the next two chapters. The bottom line is that you should have a reason for buying an investment—overhearing a conversation in the elevator doesn't count. Equally important, you should have a plan for selling the stock if necessary.

VALUE TIMING IN A BEAR MARKET

I hope you have concluded by now that I am not a fan of market timing. Almost no one with expertise in investing believes it works. However, bear markets do offer an opportunity to take advantage of bargains. We will discuss bargain shopping in detail in Chapter 15, "Fatten Up on Bear."

Down markets are very tempting times to pick up bargains—at least, so the conventional wisdom goes. What I call "value timing" is the notion that you can grab some real bargains at the bottom of the market and take a nice profit on the recovery.

Here's the problem: You can't be sure where the bottom of the market is. As the Nasdaq began dropping off its high of 5,000-plus, when would you have called the bottom of its drop?

At 4,000, a 20 percent drop?

At 3,000, a 40 percent drop?

At 2,500, a 50 percent drop?

As I write this, the Nasdaq index is barely above 2,100.

You see, the problem with fishing off the bottom is that you can never be sure where the bottom is. Few, if any, investors believed in 1999 the Nasdaq would fall this far or this fast.

The hard lesson is: *Don't invest on price alone.* If the investment doesn't make sense based on its fundamentals or, most importantly, on how it fits into your plan, don't risk your money.

ALWAYS ANOTHER DEAL

One of the other dangers of market hysteria, whether it's a bull or a bear market, is the sense that you have a "once-in-a-lifetime opportunity." If you don't act now, you will never have another chance.

The recently deceased bull market of the late 1990s may be one of the strongest in history, but it won't be the last one. There are plenty of opportunities for profitable investing every day the market is open. Some days you just have to work harder than others.

The point is that you should never jump into or out of an investment because you feel that failing to act will cost you the opportunity of a lifetime.

Don't believe it. There is always another deal.

CONCLUSION

Market timing doesn't work. Research shows you are better off invested in the market than jumping in and out in an attempt to improve your return.

Always buy and sell within an overall investing plan. You will do better and will avoid impulsive buying and selling.

CHAPTER 7

WHEN IT'S TIME
TO SELL A STOCK

The best time to sell a stock is when you have made the maximum possible return on your investment, and before it crashes. That's not so hard, is it?

Unfortunately, the market doesn't like glib answers any more than you do. Deciding when to sell is often more difficult than figuring out when to buy, but you'll hear a lot more advice on when to buy a stock than on when to sell one. Establishing a bear defense means shedding stocks that no longer fit your financial plan or move you closer to your goals. In later chapters, we will look at the process of asset allocation. Asset allocation depends on getting the correct mix of investments. Learning to sell stocks correctly is as important as learning to buy them correctly. This chapter and the next provide an introduction to the tools you need.

There is no definitive system, no "best way" to arrive at the sell decision. Investors should develop their own exit plan for getting out of a position. Without a plan, you may make snap decisions, as we discussed in the last chapter.

What follows in this chapter are summaries of some of the many strategies used by professional investors. Some of the strategies contradict others; some investors sell quickly, while others say if you buy correctly, you should almost never have to sell.

Find one that makes sense to you, or combine a few for your own plan. Either way, never buy a stock without some clear idea of when you need to get out of it. Hunches, instincts, and planetary alignments are not strategies. The key to making your strategy work is to work your strategy. That is, decide on your exit criteria and when a stock meets those points, sell and don't look back.

SELLING ON PRICE

Many successful investors have absolute rules about selling a stock whose price has fallen, and they don't vary from these rules for any reason. The rationale is that you have a better chance of long-term success if you keep your losses to a minimum.

It's hard to argue with the math: If you lose $5,000 on a stock, you have to make $5,000 plus (to account for commissions, taxes, and so on) on another stock to break even. If you had cut your loss at $1,000, then your $5,000 gain works out to be a net of $4,000 in round numbers.

What is the magic number for selling? For some investors, an 8 percent drop from the purchase price is reason to sell. Others put it at 10 percent. Either way, they don't let losses get out of hand.

C a u t i o n

> Investors use selling strategies to counteract the emotional aspect of selling. It's too easy to convince yourself that if you hold on a *little* while longer, the stock will surely bounce back.

The danger in this strategy is that unstable markets and volatile stocks may force you to sell in a correction just before the stock takes off. Of course, proponents point out that you don't *know* the stock is going to take off after a drop. It could just keep dropping, which is probably the case more often than not.

That is why this approach requires discipline. Keeping your losses to a minimum undoubtedly helps your portfolio stay profitable. If you miss a couple of big scores on stocks that turn around, that's better than watching losers sink below the horizon.

This strategy takes a very conservative approach to investing. Bear markets may drag down stocks that are fundamentally sound. This is not a strategy for "buy-and-hold" proponents, but if the thought of losing even a small amount of money is troubling, you may find it a comforting game plan.

The type of "selling on price" that most often occurs is after a stock has dropped by significant amounts and investors become frustrated and frightened. They sell at or near a bottom. A disciplined selling strategy prevents a "sell low" reaction to bad news in the market, but you might also be divesting prematurely from a fundamentally sound stock.

NOT SELLING ON PRICE

On the other hand, there are investors who say that selling on price alone is short-sighted. They suggest that unstable markets produce odd swings in price that may have nothing to do with the individual company; if nothing has fundamentally changed about why you bought the stock in the first place, then selling in a correction is wrong.

Price by itself doesn't tell you anything about the company. Bad economic or market news shows up in prices quickly. Unless something is wrong with the company, it is unlikely to keep falling for no reason. Quality companies do well over time; they're your best chance for investing success if given time to outperform the market, which they will do.

Investors who jump out of a good stock because the price dips have given up the power of time in long-term investing.

PROTECTING YOUR PROFITS

This is another "sell on price" guideline, but it's on the other side of the equation. The first one suggested you should cut your losses early. This one says don't let profits disappear.

If you have a stock that is up substantially, you may want to sell part of your holdings to take all or part of your money out. For example, you bought 1,000 shares of XYZ for $20, and a year later it is trading for $45 per share. This guideline suggests you sell 450 shares ($20,250) to recapture your original investment. Whatever the stock does after that is pure profit.

This defensive strategy keeps bears from eating your profits. It requires investors to keep a close eye on the market. If you don't get greedy, it can protect your profits from a bear's bite. If a bear forces you to sell some or all of the investment to protect your profit, be very careful how and when you reinvest the cash.

Of course, the contrary point of view suggests you let your winners run as long as they can.

IT'S GETTING TOO EXPENSIVE

This is one of the more emotionally difficult selling disciplines. It usually happens when a stock grows rapidly and the price follows. On the surface, this doesn't seem like a bad thing. You want your investments to increase in price, right?

The problem is when the company's earnings don't grow as rapidly as the stock's price. In analytical terms, the price part of the P/E ratio is growing faster than the earnings part. The P/E ratio is a simple tool that tells investors what they are paying in a stock's price for the earnings of the company.

The P/E ratio should be a low number, say, under 25. If the stock price is rising faster than the earnings, the ratio will rise. If you bought the stock because it was cheap, a rising P/E ratio is cause for concern. Overpriced stock can fall rapidly on any bad news. (Remember the Internet stock bubble, where stocks were trading with triple-digit P/E ratios.)

Plain English

The **price/earnings ratio** is computed by taking a company's stock price and dividing it by the earnings per share. The resulting number tells you roughly what investors think of the expected growth in earnings. A higher number says investors are willing to pay more for the stock because they expect higher earnings.

One advantage of a selling discipline is that it takes the emotion out of decision-making. It's too easy to get comfortable with a stock, especially one that has done well for you. However, if you're a value investor looking for a good relationship between price and earnings, this stock is off your screen. A selling plan that kicks in when a stock's P/E ratio hits a target number can help you move on to better values.

This is the value of having a plan for disposal when you buy a stock. You know exactly why you are investing, and when that reason no longer exists, you move on to another stock that meets your plan. This strategy will exit you from a stock before it reaches its top, but it will also keep you on plan, not worrying about whether the stock is going to keep rising. You don't care because you're focused on your total investing plan.

Of course, you can hedge your bets somewhat by putting in a stop-loss order on the stock. This lets the stock rise some more if there is any price increase left. However, when the stock retreats to your price, your broker or trading system executes a sell order.

Plain English ————————————————————————

Investors use a **stop-loss order** to trigger a sell order, usually to protect a profit or avoid a loss. The investor places the order below the current stock price. If the stock stays the same or rises, nothing happens. If the price falls to the stop-loss order price, it becomes a market sell order and the stock is sold without any instructions from the investor.

You should look at other valuation markers in connection with the P/E to get a better picture of the stock's situation.

REBALANCING YOUR PORTFOLIO

Rebalancing your portfolio is part of the asset-allocation process we will discuss in Chapter 9, "Asset Allocation: The Two Most Important Words in Investing," but it's worth noting here. This may be one of the toughest sell decisions, because it often involves a stock that has done really well.

You never want one stock to dominate your portfolio; however, this is what happens when you hit a big winner. Although it is tough to sell a big gainer, your portfolio is more secure when no one investment occupies a large percentage. Typically, you will want to consider selling part of any investment that exceeds 10 percent of your portfolio. Retirement accounts, such as 401(k) plans and individual retirement accounts (IRAs), are notorious for becoming unbalanced.

Caution ────────────────────────────────

> If one or two stocks heavily weight your portfolio, you are in real danger if the stocks tumble. You are particularly vulnerable during a bear market because your asset allocation is out of whack.

There are some obvious drawbacks to this rule. First, you reduce the potential for gain if the investment is still climbing. Second, you introduce some tax considerations. However, there is ample evidence that a balanced portfolio has a better chance of surviving unstable markets than one that is too dependent on a single investment. You trade some potential for growth for some protection on the downside.

THEY MISSED THEIR EARNINGS ESTIMATES

The growth or potential for growth in earnings is the most important single factor in many investors' decision to buy or sell a stock. There are a number of "earnings" numbers for each company, most of which measure the company's earnings relative to its stock price (price/earnings ratio, or P/E). However, one of the most important numbers investors watch is the earnings estimate.

Companies project their earnings out a year or so for the investing community, and are required to be as accurate as possible in these estimates. These numbers give investors an idea of what the company expects in the near future—and a warning if something is on the horizon (like lower sales) that may affect the stock price.

Stock analysts who follow individual stocks develop another set of numbers for estimates. These are usually close to the company's figures, but they may reflect a different interpretation of the economy, market, or some other factor.

Caution ────────────────────────────────

> Be aware that some companies play games to keep their earnings up when the core business is suffering. A quick look at the income statement shows where the company's income is originating, and will tell you if it's the business or the accounting department that's making money.

Every quarter, companies report their actual earnings (usually expressed as earnings per share, EPS) to the public. When a company misses these estimates more than once, it may mean that management has lost touch with the market or is having trouble controlling expenses. Either way, companies that miss estimates, especially two in a row, are good candidates for trading.

When financial news is abuzz with warnings of missed earnings and estimates of lower future earnings, beware of the bear. Nothing turns a market south faster than market leaders forecasting lower earnings. This is a good time to check your portfolio for bear-resistant products. See Part 3, "Bear Assets," for tools and strategies to protect your investments.

THEY'RE RESTATING EARNINGS

A company restates its earnings when it has reported numbers that were incorrect. Restating earnings is a way of saying, "We don't know what we're doing." You seldom hear of a company restating its earnings to a higher number.

Regulators often force companies to restate their earnings, and whether it's because of a mistake or some intentional falsehood, many investors automatically dump the stock.

THE INDUSTRY'S CHANGING

Today's superstar stock is in tomorrow's value bin. At least it seems that way sometimes. The economy is a dynamic environment. Companies that stake out a leadership role in a particular market and fail to adapt to change may find themselves out of touch.

Competition is a wonderful thing for creating new products and services. However, some companies don't evolve gracefully. They may stick to their comfort zone in spite of market changes that are moving away from their products. A company that doesn't move with the market risks its position in the industry.

> **Tip**
>
> Changes in markets, competition, and economic environments can cause problems with profits. Great companies don't just adapt to change, they lead it.

In the 1970s and 1980s, IBM dominated the mainframe computer market. They were so dominant that within corporate information-technology departments the rule was: "No one ever got fired recommending IBM." However, the market changed when personal computers and distributed processing became the rule in corporations. Ironically, IBM helped undo its position by developing the personal computer and making it popular with corporations. IBM still sells mainframe computers, but most of their business now comes from service and software for Internet solutions. They adapted to an evolving industry.

When your investment shows no sign of moving with its industry (or better yet, leading the pack), it's time to move on to another stock.

IT NO LONGER MEETS YOUR NEEDS

If you bought the stock correctly, there was a specific reason you invested your money: The stock met some need in your portfolio. When that condition changes, it may be time to move on to another investment. Here are some examples:

- You bought a growth stock that isn't growing anymore.
- You bought a market leader that has lost its dominance.
- You wanted a value stock and now it is no longer a value.

The reason you bought the stock should form the basis for measuring the investment's role in your portfolio. This is not to say you can't be pleasantly surprised when a stock seems to slip out of the role you assigned it and into one of great potential.

However, that's usually the exception. Companies go through bad times and do stupid things. Don't hesitate to cut a stock if it no longer meets your needs. When the bear comes knocking, these are among the first stocks you should consider selling and moving the cash into something more appropriate. Don't lose money on a stock you didn't want anyway. Put the money to better use, either for sitting on the sidelines waiting for the dust to clear or for picking up a stock you do want at a bargain price.

THERE ARE FUNDAMENTAL CHANGES

We live in a world that has accelerated the product cycle dramatically. Companies can no longer count on selling a proprietary product indefinitely. Manufacturers can introduce a hot new product and watch sales soar for a while, but soon the market is flooded with knockoffs and look-alike products. Proprietary products are unique. If you want their form or function, there is only one place to get it. The drug Viagra is proprietary thanks to patents. However, when the legal restraints are lifted, a number of "generic" duplicates will appear.

Personal computers used to be proprietary products of just a few manufacturers. Now dozens of companies are making computers, and they're all pretty much the same "under the hood." Personal computers have become commodities distinguished only by the shape and color of their containers.

C a u t i o n

> Profit margins drop when products become commodities. Companies that can control costs and gain market share will survive. Those that can't compete in a high-volume, low-margin arena will fail.

When a company's products become commodities, it may be time to move on. The dynamics of operating a company with a leading-edge product and a company that produces a commodity are quite different—as are the growth prospects.

MANAGEMENT IS INCOMPETENT OR CORRUPT

A company's management is often its most important asset. A great company has great management. Great management doesn't make many mistakes and they quickly reverse it when they do make a mistake. Leadership with vision and drive can make an average company a winner. Unfortunately, some CEOs lack the skill and vision to help a company succeed. Executive ego is often at the root of business blunders. The media is usually quick to point out problems in management. Too many questions about management decisions and directions may be a sign that trouble is on the horizon.

Tip

> Remember the great New Coke fiasco? The company redid the formula for the most popular soft drink in the world, only to find that everyone still wanted the "old" Coke. New is not necessarily better. The company quickly brought back the old formula—except now it was "Classic"—and moved forward.

Corrupt management is obviously a problem. It is usually too late to salvage much when the market learns that a company's management is corrupt. However, never give them a second chance.

YOU MADE A MISTAKE!

One of the most expensive mistakes you can make is to *not* admit you made a mistake with a stock. You can limit your mistakes by careful buying, but there will inevitably come a time when you kiss a frog and it turns out to be … a frog.

Ego and pride can get in the way of correcting mistakes if you are not careful. Analyzing a stock is complicated, and, in the end, you are investing in the future. Bear markets can reveal mistakes quickly. If you don't want the stock after the market returns, don't wait to unload it. That future may not turn out the way you hoped. Whatever the reasons, cut your losses on a mistake, make note of the lesson learned, and move on to the next deal.

TECHNICAL COLLAPSE

Technical analysis of stock is an exercise in identifying buying and selling points and is another whole book by itself. However, even the casual chart user can look for warning signs that a stock may be in trouble.

One major sign is a stock's price climbing rapidly for no apparent fundamental reason. You may be seeing hyperactive buying activity because the stock is the "hot" pick du jour. During the Internet bubble expansion, this was common. Remember earlier I talked about a stock that went from 20 to over 100 and back to the teens in less than a year?

T i p

> When a stock's price begins to drop on increasing daily volume, it may be time to run for cover.

Unbridled buying may be a sign that a fall is near on the first negative news. Watch your charts for double peaks where the stock has twice failed to break through to a new high.

YOU NEED THE MONEY FOR A BETTER DEAL

Obviously, this is not a completely objective decision point. If you find yourself looking at an attractive opportunity with no money to participate, take a hard look at your portfolio and see if you have a stock with less upside potential than your hot new deal. This is a somewhat risky business, but it's worth working the numbers if you believe in your new opportunity.

Before you sell one stock to buy another, you have to consider a number of assumptions and costs. First, you have to get at the true cost of the transaction, which includes calculating commissions and capital-gains taxes. Second, you need to estimate the anticipated returns from the old and new stock. Next, you must construct a "best case, worse case" comparison between the old stock and the new stock over a five-year period. At the end of five years, was it worth dumping the old stock to buy the new one? Is the worse-case scenario for the new stock better than the best-case scenario for the old stock?

A marginally better deal in the future is not worth dropping an existing investment to free money for the new deal. Be reasonably sure the new stock will *substantially* out-perform the old stock to allow for deviations from the expected returns.

Bear markets can reduce valuations on stocks to levels that make them attractive. A company that you deemed a great but expensive investment may come down to a price you like. If you think you want to own this company for the long haul, take advantage of the opportunity to dispose of a ho-hum stock for a great one.

POOR FINANCIALS

The "buy-and-hold" strategy that a number of investors advocate doesn't mean "buy and put in a drawer and forget." It's important to keep track of what's going on with your investments on at least a quarterly basis. Great companies become also-rans, and industry leaders fall from leadership roles. For a variety of reasons, balance sheets and income statements deteriorate. Understanding the reasons for declining financial strength may mean the difference between holding and selling.

For example, currency-conversion problems can hurt companies with significant international operations if a foreign country suffers problems. That can cause a company to miss earnings estimates. Understanding that the missed estimate had nothing to do with the day-to-day operations of the business can ease your mind about holding on to the stock.

Signs of weakness that raise red flags for investors are slowing sales and declines in margins. Slowing sales may mean competition is eating into the company's customer base or its products are losing market acceptance. Companies in a weakened financial condition may not be able to keep up in the technology necessary to remain competitive.

Check the financials for problems on a regular basis. More than likely you worked through the financials before you decided to invest in the company. Are the ratios still strong? Is debt rising, and, if so, why? Are profit margins evaporating?

T i p

> You should always have a standard for comparison when you invest. Whether it is a market index or other companies in the same industry, a rule to gauge performance is important.

It is also helpful to watch others in its industry. The slowdown may be across the board, not the result of some other indicator.

MERGERS AND ACQUISITIONS

Companies usually position mergers and acquisitions as being in the best interest of the two companies and their stockholders. If one of your investments is involved in a merger or acquisition, take a hard look at the resulting organization. Does it still meet your investment needs and objectives?

You can often figure much of this out before the actual transaction. Don't assume the companies know what is best for your portfolio.

DONATE TO CHARITY

Sometimes, you have the opportunity to help yourself and others at the same time. Although not an investment discipline, donating stock to charities can accomplish several goals at once.

You may be able to take a tax deduction for the value of the stock (consult with your tax advisor). At the same time, a worthy cause can use the stock for a greater good. That's not a bad deal all the way around.

FOR SOME FUN

Here's a selling tip to break every investing rule you know! Sometimes a good reason to sell a stock is to enjoy the money.

A life spent squirreling away every nickel you can misses the point. Enjoying some of the fruits of your success is perfectly acceptable, as long as you do it in a reasonable and prudent manner that does not threaten your retirement or other important financial goals.

Rewarding yourself and/or your family with a great vacation is worth every penny. Investing is a means to an end, not the end itself.

Tip
You will find numerous trading strategies in my book *Alpha Teach Yourself Investing in 24 Hours*. (Shameless plug!)

CONCLUSION

There are many reasons for selling an investment. You should know why you bought the stock and what has to happen that will trigger your sell order.

Many investing professionals counsel caution in buying to prevent panic in selling. That's good advice—unfortunately, not every investment turns out the way we planned, and bear markets can undo your best plans.

When that happens, a selling discipline will take some of the emotion out of letting go of a stock you liked but that didn't perform as expected. Find a selling strategy that makes sense to you and stick with it.

CHAPTER 8

WHEN IT'S TIME TO SELL A MUTUAL FUND

Mutual funds are supposed to be a low-maintenance investment (at least that's what their marketing material suggests). You turn your money over to professional managers who make all the hard decisions for you. For many investors, mutual funds are the perfect buy-and-hold vehicle because they give you instant diversification and expert management in one package.

We all wish it were that simple. Mutual funds are ideal investments for people who don't want to spend a great deal of time researching stocks or bonds. Individual stocks in great companies historically outperform most mutual funds; however, that assumes you buy great companies at great prices and you don't need your money during the middle of a bear market.

Buying mutual funds involves the same type of research as buying individual stocks. Like stocks, mutual funds can and do go bad for a variety of reasons. As we found in the previous chapter on selling stocks, there is much more information available on *buying* a mutual fund than on *selling* one. Investors make the same selling mistakes with mutual funds as they do with stocks. In some ways, it is harder with funds because we come to rely on professional managers to overcome any problems. However, there are problems that managers can't or won't overcome that signal it's time to move on to another investment. Even market professionals running mutual funds have trouble in bear markets. Don't assume that they have all the answers.

A well-thought-out selling strategy is an important tool in your investing arsenal. Your selling strategy will tell you when it's time to sell and will take some of the emotion out of the situation. In this chapter, we'll look at some strategies, and at those situations when it is appropriate to sell a fund and move on to something else. You will find many of the conditions similar to the ones outlined in the previous chapter. However, some conditions are unique to mutual funds. (Note: When I refer to stocks, bonds, or cash in this chapter, I mean stock mutual funds, bond funds, or money-market funds.)

THE FUND LOSES TOO MUCH

This may seem like a "no brainer," but it's a little more complicated than it might initially appear. Of course, you can and should set some performance goals. The catch comes in setting the goals to an appropriate standard.

Mutual funds represent a sector or segment of the market, such as growth stock funds or small cap funds. Unlike individual stocks, you can measure funds against other similar funds or indexes.

- **Growth stock funds.** Mutual funds that invest in growing companies look for stock price appreciation. Growth companies are typically younger firms that put growth above current profits.
- **Small cap funds.** Mutual funds that invest in smaller companies hope they will eventually become bigger. These include very young companies and most recently, high tech companies. Investors are hoping to find another Microsoft before it becomes a true growth stock.
- **Large cap funds.** Mutual funds that invest in large companies are looking for the leaders in different industry segments. Market segment leaders are always large companies.

However, you buy mutual funds, like individual stocks, to fill a particular niche in your investment plan. A fund that is at or near the top of its sector but still losing ground may not be a candidate for selling.

Mutual funds use market indexes to measure their performance. For example, large cap mutual funds usually use the S&P 500 index as the target they want to beat. The S&P 500 represents the largest 500 companies in the market. There are also many resources on the Internet that measure large cap funds against each other. The best source for this information is Morningstar.com.

During a bear market, you want your fund to do as well as or better than its peers. If it is not, that may be a signal to sell. On the other hand, if funds in the sector are posting double-digit gains and your fund is losing money, it may be time to move on to another fund that meets your portfolio needs.

THE FUND GAINS TOO MUCH

Can your investments ever gain too much? That doesn't seem a likely reason to dump a fund, but there are some valid reasons. If your fund is the opposite of the last example—earning double-digit returns while its peers languish on the sidelines—something is probably wrong.

What could be wrong with posting big gains? The problem could be that you don't own what you think you do. Mutual funds can be very creative with their names. Just because the fund name indicates it is one type of fund doesn't mean it *is* that type of fund.

Mutual fund companies are not above stepping outside the niche their name implies to boost returns. Morningstar.com has some excellent tools for analyzing a mutual fund based on what it actually does as opposed to what the name might imply.

Tip

> The best defense against a bear market is a well-diversified portfolio appropriate to your age and financial goals. Part 3, "Bear Assets," will help you design a portfolio that meets these qualifications.

The problem with this situation is that your asset allocation could be all out of alignment because the fund you thought was covering one area is actually overlapping somewhere else. This may leave your portfolio vulnerable without you knowing it. Morningstar.com has an excellent free service that will help you "x-ray" your mutual fund to see exactly what makes it tick.

You may not need to sell a misnamed fund, especially if it is doing very well. You can shift it in your asset allocation plan to the area where it really belongs and find a new fund to cover the now-vacant sector.

THERE IS A STRATEGY CHANGE

This situation is similar to the one above except there is a conscious effort by the fund manager to change the focus of the fund.

A manager might change strategies for a variety of reasons. Maybe a new fund's original concept just wasn't working, or it was unable to attract new investors. Funds that focus on a particular industry segment may find that consolidation leaves them with too few companies to sustain a fund.

Whatever the reason, this is an important time to reevaluate why you own this fund and whether its new strategy will serve your needs.

UNDERPERFORMING FUNDS

Not all managers are equal. Some managers can look at the same industry segment and carve out a profitable mutual fund while other managers can't seem to find the handle.

Fund managers are extremely important; a later section of this chapter is devoted to mutual fund managers. If your fund is consistently in the bottom half of its peer group, that may be a sell signal.

Underperforming is not the same as losing too much money, which we discussed earlier. An underperforming fund may actually be making money. However, if it is consistently in the bottom half of its peer group, that isn't good enough. You shouldn't settle for an underperforming fund when there are usually many others to take its place.

I wouldn't be too concerned about slips in performance over one or two quarters. Any manager can have some slippage from time to time.

Caution

Jumping from one fund to another for a few one hundredths of a point is a losing game. Fees and taxes will consume any additional gain in return.

YOU SET NEW GOALS

You will have better results over the long-term by buying and holding on to quality funds. However, your life is not static. Things change, and you can develop new financial goals and obligations. You certainly need to reassess your portfolio under these circumstances. At various stages, such as retirement, you should rethink your holdings. There are times to be very aggressive and other times when that is not prudent.

Asset allocation is the process of dividing your portfolio among stocks, bonds, and cash based on your stage in life and financial goals. In Chapter 9, "Asset Allocation: The Two Most Important Words in Investing," we will talk more about asset allocation.

Tip

There is no magic formula for asset allocation. There are some suggestions, but as with any investment advice you should temper them with your own tolerance for risk and investment goals.

REBALANCING YOUR PORTFOLIO

This selling strategy recognizes that, over time, funds that do exceptionally well may occupy a greater percentage of your portfolio than is appropriate.

For example, you may want your portfolio to reflect the following allocation:

60 percent stocks

30 percent bonds

10 percent cash

A large run-up in one of these areas could throw your portfolio out of balance. If you had owned a fund focused on Internet/tech stocks in the late 1990s, you might have experienced a big increase. This increase could result in your portfolio looking like this:

80 percent stocks

15 percent bonds

5 percent cash

You can get your portfolio back in sync by selling off some stock funds (laggards would be a good choice) or by putting more money into bond funds and money market funds.

Bear markets are prime candidates for throwing your portfolio out of balance. Take the time to reexamine your position or you may find your diversified portfolio shield has some holes. It is important to watch your tax situation when selling funds. Unfortunately, the tax liabilities funds generate have to do with how often the manager buys and sells within the fund. Funds distribute capital-gains taxes to shareholders, usually toward the end of the year. Selling before the distribution may make sense from a tax point of view, but, as always, consult your tax professional for advice.

AVOIDING OVERLAP

This selling strategy follows rebalancing your portfolio to return the assets to the proper proportions. Mutual funds come in many flavors and with names that don't necessarily reflect their composition.

> **Caution**
>
> One of the major strengths of diversification is that parts of your portfolio will react differently under the same market conditions. If your funds overlap, you may not have the diversification you thought.

If you're not careful, you may find that you own several funds that are investing in the same types of companies and possibly even the same companies. This defeats the purpose of diversification. You can use free tools on Morningstar.com to analyze individual mutual funds and compare several funds for overlap. Morningstar categorizes funds by what stocks they actually buy, as opposed to how the fund might categorize itself. This way you get an objective view of a fund and can decide if it still fits your portfolio.

Another service from Morningstar called, appropriately, X-Ray can look at several funds and compare holdings. A premium service shows you where two or more funds overlap in holdings. A quick comparison of two funds, Oppenheimer Main Street Growth and Income A Fund, and the Domini Social Equity Fund, reveals that both funds have significant holdings in some major large growth stocks. Owning these two funds would not satisfy your diversification needs; the overlap between them indicates that they would probably move in the same direction in response to market conditions. This would be a time to sell one of the funds and move on to another sector in your portfolio. This can be a rude awakening during a bear market. Overlapping funds move in the same direction at just the time you need diversification the most.

THE MANAGER LEAVES

Managers play an important role in the life of a mutual fund—so much so that when one leaves it is an automatic sell signal to many investors. There are many legendary managers of funds with impressive records of consecutive market-beating gains. When they move on or retire, the funds often flounder through one or more new managers. Just as some horseracing fans bet on the jockey, some investors watch where winning managers go and follow with their money.

A departing manager is not an automatic sell for all investors; however, it is always a heads-up that things may change. There are a couple of exceptions to the automatic sell rule. The first is that passively managed funds are much less dependent on the manager. For example, an S&P 500 index fund requires much fewer manager decisions than an aggressive stock fund. Index funds follow a rigid set of guidelines that take much of the decision-making out of the manager's hands. A manager leaving may not hurt this type of passively managed fund.

The second situation where a manager's departure may not have a significant impact is with large mutual fund families. Companies that manage 25 or more funds usually have large and talented staffers who can take over when a manager leaves. When you have funds with a smaller management company, you need to be more concerned about the departure of a manager.

Tip

It's not a bad idea to keep an eye on a hot manager who leaves one fund for another. If he or she is taking over a similar fund, it might be worth it to consider following the manager with your money.

THE FUND GETS TOO BIG

Size in the investing community has its advantages but also its disadvantages. Some funds have a difficult time maneuvering when they grow too big. During intense periods like the Internet/tech stock explosion in the late 1990s, money poured into the market in unprecedented amounts. Mutual funds that invested in large cap, growth stocks had little trouble investing the money. However, some of the small funds that targeted small cap, tech stocks were also flooded with money. The problem they faced was where to put all the money flowing into the fund.

Small cap, tech stocks are highly vulnerable even in the best of times. Managers of these funds usually face two choices: They could broaden the holdings outside the small-cap stocks, or they could close the fund to new investors.

Funds that require nimbleness and flexibility are most at risk from becoming too large. These funds are big, fat targets for bear markets. Big funds that must sell off stocks during a declining market may add pressure to the sell-off in a bear market.

Tip

Mutual funds that focus in "hot" sectors, like the Internet/tech funds, may not perform as well as the market. When the underlying stocks move, it is usually all in the same direction.

PROTECTING YOUR PROFITS

There is a great debate between investors who believe you should let your profits run and those who feel it is wise to take some or all of your profits to protect your invested capital. The folks who believe you should let your profits run see no reason to cut short a profitable investment. Folks on the other side feel they could reinvest some or all of the profits elsewhere to better use.

Tip ———————————————————————————————

> If you can protect a profit in a bear market by selling some or all of a winner, you can put that money to use by picking up a fund that is currently depressed but has great potential.

For example, if you had a $5,000 profit on a $5,000 original investment, they would suggest to take out the original $5,000 and reinvest it in another fund. The $5,000 remaining in the fund is pure profit, and they are free to withdraw it or let it continue to grow.

Like individual stocks, mutual fund profits need protection, and a bear market may be the best time to take some profit and run to safer havens until the market settles down.

POOR MANAGEMENT

Poor management is one of the best reasons to sell a mutual fund. There is no reason to stick with a fund that has poor management. A poorly managed fund is not going to get any better except by luck, and that's not very comforting for investors.

A poorly managed fund will exhibit some or all of the following characteristics:

* A history of underperforming similar types of funds or indexes
* Higher than normal fees
* Higher than normal turnover (buying and selling stocks)
* Confused signals on the direction the fund is taking

MISTAKE AT PURCHASE

The Securities and Exchange Commission has expressed concern over the way management companies name mutual funds. They feel that some of the names are misleading investors to believe they are buying one type of fund, when that is not the case. You wouldn't be the first investor who thought they were buying a value fund, only to discover most of the investments were in growth stocks. You also wouldn't be the only investor who bought a fund only to realize that a fund they already owned covered the same type of stocks.

It is never a mistake to correct a mistake. If you picked the wrong fund for your asset-allocation plan, you are vulnerable until you correct the mistake.

YOU NEED MONEY FOR A BETTER DEAL

It is not to your long-term benefit to jump in and out of mutual funds, although this seems more popular than ever. Mutual funds have made it easy to switch funds within families of funds.

However, there are times when you have spotted an attractive situation and need money to take advantage of the opportunity. This is a good time to check the performance of your funds and weed out any that are underperforming or lagging in some manner.

Before you dump one fund for another, be sure the potential return of the new fund is significantly greater than that of the old fund. If not, you may be better off sitting tight. Bear market are great times to pick up funds that have had their share values beaten down but remain solid investments.

FUND IS TOO VOLATILE

Some investors have a difficult time accepting losses. If this describes you, don't feel like you have to own any fund whose price fluctuates wildly. If your stomach is not up to some gut-wrenching volatility, you need a fund that is less explosive and more predictable. The point of investing is to secure a financial future; it may not be worth it to you to wrestle with a highly volatile stock fund just to achieve some financial goal.

Many funds offer very attractive returns without betting the farm on every trade. Stick with what makes you comfortable, and don't worry about not owning the latest and greatest fund.

Tip ——————————————————————————————

There are too many good funds for you to be stuck with one that churns your stomach with its wild swings. If you are losing sleep over a fund, lose the fund.

DONATE TO CHARITY

Are you sitting on a mutual fund that is not really going anywhere? Why not consider donating it to a charitable cause? There are some good "win-win" reasons for making donations. More than likely, you can take a deduction for the appreciated value of the fund, and the charity gets an asset they can let grow or cash in for current needs.

FOR SOME FUN

Never let investing become so all-consuming that you have no time to enjoy life. There is no good reason you shouldn't enjoy the fruits of your labor from time to time. As long as you aren't threatening your retirement or other important financial goal, take some of your hard-earned and invested money and do something good for yourself.

A family vacation or other diversion may be the best investment you can make. Selling a fund is a serious step, but rewarding yourself and your family with a vacation or some other luxury makes working hard worthwhile.

CONCLUSION

You're clearly better off in the market than out of it, even in a bear market. That doesn't mean you should be stuck with funds that aren't pulling their weight.

Careful planning and research when you purchase a fund eliminates many problems down the road. However, life and the markets have a way of not following your most careful plan. When that happens, you need an exit strategy. This plan should be in place when you buy the fund and not made up as you go.

Selling can be harder emotionally than buying because, in some cases, we have to confront our own failings and put our ego aside. An exit strategy that makes sense to you will help take some of the emotion out of selling a fund you may like, but that no longer fits your needs.

PART 3

BEAR ASSETS

This part of the book focuses on the practice of asset allocation. Many investment professionals believe properly allocating your assets (stocks, bonds, and cash) is more important than the actual asset selection. I'm not sure I would go quite that far, but if you don't practice asset allocation, you're leaving your portfolio vulnerable to bear attacks.

We will also look at how asset allocation works during periods of recession, inflation, and deflation, and how different types of stocks and bonds respond to bear markets and economic downturns. Finally, we'll take a brief look at the different sectors of the economy and how they fare in a bear market.

CHAPTER 9

ASSET ALLOCATION: THE TWO MOST IMPORTANT WORDS IN INVESTING

Simply put, asset allocation is how you split up your portfolio among the three asset classes: stocks, bonds, and cash. Investors plan their asset-allocation strategy to achieve the best returns in any circumstances, which means an asset-allocation strategy should be dynamic and subject to change as other factors change.

You need to know up front that no magic formula will completely protect you from every bear market. Asset allocation is as much an art as it is a science; there is no single "right" way to do it. (In fact, some proponents believe you should only consider stocks and bonds in the scheme.) Your goal is to achieve the best return for your individual situation in the present market, which is not the same as achieving the best possible return.

Asset allocation isn't particularly *hard,* but it's complicated because it's composed of many variables. The difficulty in identifying a bear market in advance further compounds the problem. The "super bear" market we discussed in Chapter 1, "Bear Markets," was a good case in point. There was no perfect allocation of assets that completely protected investors. The best investors could hope for was to not lose as much as the rest of the market; even converting every-thing to cash wasn't the answer because inflation was eating away at the value of everything.

In this chapter, we are going to look at asset allocation in a general context. As we move deeper into the book, the focus will become more and more specific. In this discussion, the terms "stocks," "bonds," and "cash" refer to the class alone: When I use the term stocks, unless other-wise noted, I mean both individual stocks and stock funds. Same with bonds—I am referring to individual bonds or bond funds. Cash can be any form of savings, from money market funds to money market ac-counts. This is not the cash you should have on-hand for emergencies, usually enough to cover three to six months' expenses. (When it's impor-tant to make distinctions, I will do so.)

ASSET ALLOCATION IN CONTEXT

Many market professionals believe that getting your asset allocation right is more important than the individual assets you buy. The theory is that different asset classes react differently under the same market conditions, so the right allocation will flatten out the peaks and valleys in your port-folio over time.

By definition, this means you will not get the "best" return that cor-rectly timing the market brings—but we've already seen that no one can consistently time the market correctly, and you will also avoid the worst losses.

T i p

> If you have substantial assets, or find this all too overwhelming, you may want to engage a financial planner to help you with your asset alloca-tion. If you finish this book, you'll be ready to ask the important ques-tions an advisor should answer.

MORE THAN DIVERSIFICATION

Asset allocation is diversification on steroids. Both strategies offer some protection in an unstable market. Diversification looks at spreading your investments over different assets. Asset allocation takes that a step further and suggests how much of your portfolio to put in each asset class and how to split it up within each class.

For example, diversification might suggest you have 75 percent of your assets in stocks. Asset allocation takes that total investment in stocks and structures the percentage of domestic, foreign, growth, value, and so on.

Some market professionals don't make a distinction between diversification and asset allocation. You may read information about diversification that sounds just like what this book says about asset allocation. The specific terms are less important than the strategy behind them.

INVESTING IN HISTORY

There is no shortage of market soothsayers quick to tell you how you should have profited in the latest market move. Clearly, it's easy to know where to invest in the historical market: When the Nasdaq was up 87-plus percent in one year, where should you have invested your money?

Of course, that's not the whole picture. Imagine that the 87-plus percent increase occurred in one 12-month period and had a straight-line growth rate from the beginning to the end. A graph would show the line originating at the bottom left and going straight across to the top right, as shown here. Almost any point along that line would have been an okay place to buy because the market was always going up.

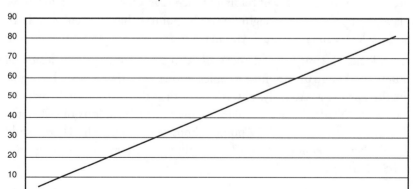

Market Up 87 Percent in One Year

The following graph shows the same final result: The market ended up 87 for the year. However, there was only a brief period at the beginning of the year when you could get in for less than 87. Any other entry point and you would have broken even, at best, unless you sold before the year was out.

Market Up 87 Percent in One Year

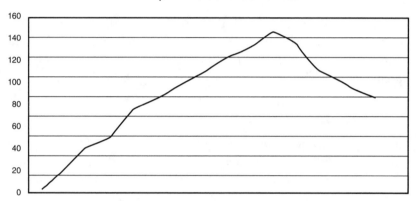

Looking back, it's easy to see where you should have entered the market. The same strategy would not have worked for both markets represented by the two charts. Unfortunately, you can't invest in history, and neither chart tells us anything about how the next year is going to look.

Although these charts are obviously for illustration, they make a point: The market doesn't move in a straight line like the first chart. The following chart is very real. It shows the closing of the Nasdaq Composite Index on the first day of trading of each year. Of course, with just three data points, we do get straight lines. The point is that your entry and exit points determine how much you make or lose.

This looks so simple—and that's the danger of dealing with historical numbers. The market almost doubles in one year, then loses all its gains in the next year. Actually, it was even worse than that. On March 10, 2000, the Nasdaq closed at 5048. In the last nine months of 2000, the Nasdaq Composite lost 2757 points, almost 55 percent. This chart should be a sobering reminder to those who thought the market could go nowhere but up forever.

Nasdaq Composite

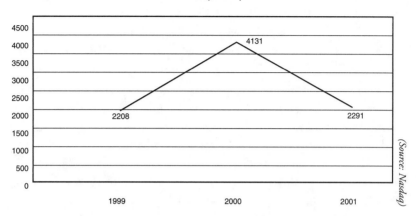

If you had the time, patience, and data, you could construct a bear-proof marketing plan for this time frame—but we aren't going to see this market again. And in the unlikely event that we did see this market again, you wouldn't know it until it was already over. Looking at historical data can help you understand how different asset classes perform under different circumstances, but it's impossible to know when those circumstances will appear again.

SETTING REALISTIC GOALS

Unless you just put your portfolio on automatic pilot, you should expect to do better than the market (S&P 500 index). The problem arises when investors try to wring every last penny out of the market. The market timers we discussed in Chapter 6, "Market Timing: The Two Most Dangerous Words in Investing," attempt to get in at the bottom and out at the top of a market. Very few do, and then only rarely.

If you aim for returns above the market, over time you will do quite well. If you aim for huge returns, over time you will probably do worse than the market.

I've told the following story in other books, so if it seems familiar, "bear" with me. One year, when I was a youngster playing Little League baseball, my friend's father decided to help the two of us with our hitting before the season. He had played major league baseball in his younger days, so he knew what he was doing. We worked on our hitting for several weeks, and his instruction took hold.

My batting average that year was a league-leading .797. For you non-baseball fans, a .300 batting average is good for professionals. Another way to look at it is for every 10 times I came to bat, I got a hit eight times.

The professional had taught me to focus on just making contact with the ball. That season I never hit a home run, and I had only one triple. In fact, most of my hits were singles. The point is that my "unspectacular" year was the best in the league, because I focused on small gains rather than large ones.

The analogy isn't perfect, but the lesson is right on: Aim for better-than-average gains, and over the long term you have a much better chance for success than trying to hit a home run every time. Market timers swing for home runs. Investors focus on their long-term success.

VARIABLES OF ASSET ALLOCATION

Asset allocation is more than just dividing your portfolio into different asset classes. The two main variables of asset allocation are risk tolerance and time horizon, and these variables prevent a single asset allocation that is right for every investor. The asset allocation for a 30-year-old single woman may be quite different from the mix that is right for a 60-year-old man hoping to retire soon.

Your risk tolerance will either open or close some possibilities in asset allocation and selection. Your time horizon also has a tremendous impact on finding the right asset mix.

Tip

> Your financial goals will require different asset-allocation models. Don't be concerned if one model is radically different from the others because of the time involved.

Many investors have more than one financial goal (I assume retirement is a common goal). College for the kids, a vacation home, or other goals will need their own asset allocation because of the time frame and definable financial needs. Let's look at these variables individually.

RISK TOLERANCE

Risk tolerance describes an investor's willingness to take risks with investments. Higher-risk investments should offer higher potential returns than low-risk products, and with the higher potential return comes the possibility of a larger loss if things go badly. There's nothing wrong with having a small percentage of your portfolio in higher-risk products, but there's no rule that says you have to.

The meltdown of the Nasdaq and Internet/tech stocks that began in the spring of 2000 illustrates an important point about risk tolerance: A super-heated bull market masks high-risk investments. The market allowed investors who normally would avoid stocks with huge P/E ratios to convince themselves the stocks were really not that risky. When the market started crumbling, investors couldn't believe the bull run was over and ignored normal sell indicators, hoping the market would reverse course and return to previous heights and beyond. Investors with large positions in this sector saw their holdings vaporize and were tempted to take even greater risks to get back their lost wealth.

Of course, the market didn't force investors to do any of these things. That is why in Chapters 7, "When It's Time to Sell a Stock," and 8, "When It's Time to Sell a Mutual Fund," we discussed the importance of planning your exit and sticking to your plan. A well-thought-out asset-allocation plan places you in investments that meet your risk-tolerance levels. Plan your exit strategy in advance, and avoid the emotional traps of dealing with a loss.

TIME HORIZON

Another critical factor in your asset-allocation plan is the time horizon you have to meet your financial goal. Your time horizon and risk tolerance work together to give you an indication of which investments are appropriate and which are not. As we saw in Chapter 1, bear markets can last months if not years. It may take the market years to recover ground lost in a bear market.

Caution

Time can be your best friend in investing because it compounds its power. However, it can work against you if a rapidly approaching financial goal is threatened.

Aggressive growth stocks may be very appropriate as part of a young person's portfolio, but very inappropriate for someone entering retirement and adverse to risk. They can be the first to stumble if the total economy or their sector begins to slow, which is what began in the spring of 2000 with the Internet/tech stocks.

Five years is about the minimum you should give yourself to recover from a bear market. This means as you approach retirement, you need to adjust your asset allocation for protection first and growth second.

The problem with asset-allocation models of the past is they did not anticipate people living as long as they do today. Many older models would have pulled you out of all but the most conservative, income-producing stocks as you neared retirement. Today, people who retire at age 65 may enjoy another 15 to 20 years. That's too long to be absent from stocks, even some growth issues.

Tip

The increased life span modern medicine is giving us has radically changed and will continue to change many of the social and financial structures of our society. For example, longevity is a major reason Social Security is threatened.

Yes, you might miss some of the big rallies, but you'll stay above the deep valleys—at least that's the goal. As you approach some financial goal, think about how to protect those funds. Chapter 13, "Age-Appropriate Strategies," focuses more on the issue of using asset allocation later in life.

THE RIGHT MIX

Most folks consider finding the right mix a matter of assigning percentages to stocks, bonds, and cash. Older allocation models followed this principal. One common rule still talked about is to subtract your age from 100 to equal what percentage of your portfolio should be in stocks. For example, a 60-year-old would have 40 percent invested in stocks under this formula. However, a person this old may have 20 to 25 years still to go.

The biggest financial threat to retirees is that they will outlive their money. Even if inflation holds at 3 percent per year, what costs a dollar today will cost $1.80 in 20 years. They can invest too conservatively and have to drain their principal to cover rising costs. On the other hand, they can be too aggressive and lose ground in a substantial bear market. Some financial-planning professionals suggest that the formula be updated to 110 minus your age. This supposedly addresses the issue of longer life spans.

While there is much agreement that asset allocation is important, there is no such agreement on how to slice up the pie.

Caution

It is not unheard of for market professionals to suggest that asset allocation is unnecessary. What they mean is if you do nothing else but watch the market all day, and have been doing it for 30 years, you probably can get by without asset allocation. For the rest of us, it's extremely important.

Another approach to finding the right mix is more concerned with the relationship between aggressive investments and conservative investments. This makes a lot of sense when some bond types act more aggressively than stocks at times. The general rule is that individual stocks are more risky than bonds, which are more risky than cash, but there's less truth to that statement than some want to admit.

It may be easier for you to think in terms of more or less aggressive, or you may find the percentages work better. Either way, your asset-allocation plan needs to reflect a degree of risk that is comfortable for you and appropriate for your financial goals.

THE BALANCING ACT

As I mentioned earlier, asset allocation is a dynamic process. That doesn't mean you need to tweak it every week or even every month. You should review your asset allocation plan at least once a year, or more often if there has been a major shift in the market.

For example, if you were carrying 75 percent stocks before the Nasdaq collapsed, you may find that your stock percentage is 60 percent or less. When this happens, it's time to rebalance your portfolio. You can do this one of several ways:

- Add money to stocks. This is easy if you have the extra cash available to bring up the percentage by buying more stocks.
- Sell some bonds to reduce its percentage, and use the cash to raise the percentage of stocks.
- If you include cash in your mix, use some of it to purchase stocks.

If you sell some bonds and use the money to buy stocks, be careful of the tax implications. Taxes aren't an issue if you're trading in a retirement account, but if not, look for bonds or bond funds with a loss or the smallest gain to reduce your tax hit.

If mutual funds are part of your portfolio (and they should be), make sure you don't defeat yourself by buying funds that buy the same stocks. Two different funds with "growth" in their names may have very different investment styles; even worse, two funds may sound completely different but are investing in the same stocks. Your goal of diversification is defeated when this happens. Morningstar.com assigns mutual funds to specific categories based on what the fund actually buys, rather than its name, so that's a good place to check. You can go even deeper and look at the major holdings of each fund to see if there is any overlap.

CHANGING THE MIX

You should change your allocation mix in small increments over time. Think of a knob you can gently turn to move your portfolio from aggressive to conservative. You can monitor the different assets on a regular basis and make changes when appropriate, such as when a mutual fund just isn't working.

Changing the actual mix is appropriate as you get older and your financial goals change. It is also appropriate in response to or in anticipation of a major shift in market direction—in other words, if you fear a bear is lurking around the corner. The next three chapters discuss allocation in different bear markets.

CONCLUSION

The right asset allocation for you is a combination of your tolerance for risk and your time horizon to reach a financial goal.

Asset allocation will not guarantee you a profit or prevent a loss, but it *will* help you achieve reasonable goals in unstable markets and is your best protection against a bear market.

CHAPTER 10

ASSET ALLOCATION IN A RECESSION BEAR MARKET

The unraveling of the stock market beginning in the spring of 2000 started a long slide that many thought was just a correction. After all, we were on a decade-long bull-market high, and nothing could stop the momentum of the Internet/tech juggernaut. There was a brief rally in the summer months, but by September, the Nasdaq was on a roller coaster going down.

Meanwhile, the economy kept humming along at a torrid pace. Clearly, a recession didn't cause this bear market. Not until later in 2000 did the "R" word begin to pop up in news stories on the economy, and even then, terms like "soft landing" were preferred over "slowdown." But a few analysts were beginning to worry that the soft landing might turn into a hard landing.

The damage continued into 2001, when signs of a recession began to get more attention. How should investors prepare their portfolios?

RECESSIONS

A recession is negative economic growth for two consecutive quarters. The economic indicators we looked at in Chapter 4, "Economic Indicators," can point to signs of a slowdown in economic growth that will affect future earnings. To the stock market, however, those indicators are just a record of the past—it's more concerned with how bad news from economic indicators is going to shape the *future*.

When economists officially proclaim a recession, it's like closing the barn door after the cows get out. Whether a slowdown technically qualifies as a recession doesn't really matter to investors, except that use of the "R" word tends to further erode consumer confidence.

C a u t i o n

> There's an old saying in the stock market that the majority is wrong most of the time. You might also say that when the herd starts moving in one direction, it's hard to change course. No one wants to be a party pooper when things are going well, despite signs that the party is about to end—then suddenly, everyone leaves at once.

It may be helpful to remember that a recession isn't the *cause* of a slowing economy—it is the *result* of a slowing economy. A slowing economy affects the stock market in adverse ways: it eats into corporate profits, which makes future earnings suspect, which causes investors to reduce the price they are willing to pay.

Our last recession began in 1990; ironically, during the beginning of a bull market and the end of a bear. The conditions that shaped that recession had less of an impact on the market than many anticipated.

WHAT HAPPENS WHEN THE ECONOMY GOES SOUTH

A slowdown in the economy is more than just some numbers that economists record: It's a tangible indicator of weakness, and some would suggest, a natural part of the economic cycle.

Recessions and economic slowdowns don't have to follow an identical pattern. Some recessions may include rapid inflation, while others might see the opposite—deflation. Here are some of the factors found in recessions and how they might affect the stock market.

SLOWING GROWTH

The gross national product is the sum of all goods and services produced by the country. When this measure declines for two consecutive quarters, economists announce that we are in a recession.

When the market for goods and services is contracting, businesses don't grow as fast (if at all) as in an expanding economy. Investors are always buying either future growth or earnings. A company that has been growing at 20 percent per year might only achieve 10 percent growth thanks to a contracting economy. This slowing growth rate will usually lower stock prices.

Companies that produce discretionary (nonessential) consumer items are among the first hit. Other casualties include companies that provide goods and services to other companies and the more risky, smaller companies. Generally, companies involved in staples, like food, hold up better than the market. People don't stop buying toilet paper during a recession.

INFLATION CONCERNS

Inflation may or may not accompany a recession. In fact, as we'll see later in the chapter, inflation can lead the economy into a recession. Neither inflation nor its cure (higher interest rates) are good for the stock market. Inflation concerns mean interest-rate hikes are likely, which isn't good for business or the stock market. Increased borrowing expense directly affects earnings and growth.

Bonds also tend to do poorly in periods of rising interest rates. Other interest-rate sensitive sectors include financial services, construction, and manufacturing concerns. Mutual funds that focus on hard assets like real estate may do better than the rest of the market during periods of rising inflation.

RISING UNEMPLOYMENT

As businesses slow down in response to the economy, companies lay off workers and create fewer new jobs. Rising unemployment isn't always a bad thing from the employer's point of view. It means there may be more potential employees for those companies still expanding, and wages are driven down by the demand for jobs.

On the other hand, fewer consumers are spending as freely as in the past. This has a direct affect on producers of discretionary items, such as televisions and sports equipment.

Tip

Companies like computer makers rely on business expansion to create demand for their product. When things begin to slow, this business model suffers almost immediately.

DECLINING CONSUMER SPENDING

Consumer spending is a powerful engine for our economy. Consumer spending is so important to our economy that it can lead into a recession by itself. When consumers are nervous about inflation or job security, they tend to put off nonessential purchases.

Declining spending can be like tipping over the first domino in a row and watching the chain reaction. Reduced spending hurts retailers, which causes them to lay off workers and cut back on new orders. Wholesalers then cut orders from the manufacturers, and manufacturers reduce production and cut staff.

Nothing does very well in a reduced consumer-spending cycle. Companies that make "luxury" items like boats, sports equipment, and home electronics suffer from declining consumer spending, along with clothing makers and entertainment industries. Utilities and basic transportation companies may have a better chance of not losing ground in this environment than other industries.

Tip

Investors used to consider utilities to be stable, conservative investments that paid dividends, but were otherwise boring. Don't make that assumption anymore. Deregulation and other market forces have changed the face of some utilities dramatically. Bad business decisions make some utilities risky investments at best.

OTHER RECESSION RAMIFICATIONS

No two recessions are exactly alike, because no two economies are exactly like. The conditions associated with recession that we've discussed so far are the primary ones you will normally see, but there are other factors to deal with also.

For example, rising fuel costs are not a result of a recession, but they can certainly contribute to a recession. Rising fuel costs over several quarters is always a cause of concern, adding extra expense to just about every industry in the country, figuring into virtually every product and service as well as family budgets. As such, they are highly inflationary.

Prices for gasoline and diesel fuel rose dramatically in the late 1990s and into 2001. Where I live, gasoline has jumped from a low of $1 per gallon in 1998 to almost $2 per gallon in the summer of 2000. It has momentarily settled at around $1.50 per gallon. That's a tremendous increase in a very short period. Businesses and families have had to absorb those costs into their budgets, and most families don't have a way to pass those costs on to someone else.

Businesses restrain from passing on all extra costs for fear of pricing their products and services out of the market, but if they can't pass on all of the extra fuel costs, it comes out of earnings.

ASSET ALLOCATION IN A RECESSION BEAR MARKET

In the best of all worlds, you would see the recession bear market coming and switch out of aggressive growth stocks and into holdings that are more defensive. However, as we have already discussed, identifying a bear market is neither easy nor straightforward. Once you find yourself in a bear market, it may be too late to switch investments without taking a loss.

You could adopt a permanently defensive posture, but you'd be giving up most of your upside in a bull market. There are dangers in being too conservative just as there are in being too aggressive.

What you do about asset allocation in a recession bear market and how you do it is largely a matter of personal preference, risk tolerance, and time horizon. In later chapters, we will look in detail at specific asset-allocation strategies for a variety of circumstances. It will be impossible to describe an asset-allocation model for every situation, but some examples can help you formulate your own program.

MODIFIED MARKET TIMING

If you enjoy following the market, you may be interested in an asset-allocation plan that comes close to market timing without stepping over the line. The goal is to leave your growth stocks in the market as long as you can before they begin to turn down. Letting your profits run is a great way to build wealth fast in the market, but if you sit and watch the market crater and do nothing, you're leaving all your profits on the table.

This approach requires a disciplined selling strategy and a willingness to stay on top of market and economic indicators. You need to keep an eye out for signs of a bear market emerging from or before a recession; it can be on top of you in a moment.

Tip

Active investors love to trade. However, for most of us we simply don't have the time or expertise to be active traders, so it's better to buy and hold or leave the trading to mutual fund managers.

You set sell points at some level above your purchase price and the market price. If you are optimistic about the market and economy, set the sell points fairly high. Once you see the economy heading south, move your sell points just under the market price to protect any profits in the investment.

This may sound easy, but it's not. Most investors who try this strategy will be worse off at the end of the bear market than when they started. You'll either bail out too early and miss more growth or stay too late and find others looking for safety have already bid up the defensive stocks you wanted.

As you can tell, I'm not a big fan of this strategy. It's too reliant on you correctly predicting a bear market recession. What if the recession develops, but the bear market doesn't? You also have to consider the possibility that a bear market will precede a recession.

A DEFENSIVE STRATEGY

There are always analysts who are sure a bear market is around every corner, and with signs of a recession on the horizon, they will run for cover. They suggest you adopt a permanent "prepare for the worst" portfolio anticipating a recession bear market.

A defensive strategy would focus on traditionally more stable income-producing investments such as utilities, bonds, and preferred stock. Growth investments would only occupy a small portion of the total portfolio.

Tip

> The object of investing is to make your money work for you. You are generally better off in the end staying in the market than jumping in and out of investments.

The problem here is obvious. This asset-allocation plan would have watched the biggest bull market in history from the sidelines. If you don't give yourself the opportunity to profit in the market, why bother to invest at all?

A MIDDLE-GROUND APPROACH

If the Modified Market Timing and Defensive Strategy approaches represent the extremes, where is the middle ground?

A recession bear market presents a special challenge in that very few sectors are going to do well. As noted earlier, staples such as food products may fair better than other sectors. Hard-asset based investments such as real estate provide no help.

You will find that much advice on bear markets ends up in the same place: Do nothing and wait for the market to come back. It may be best to focus on maintaining your position rather than racking up gains. If your holdings are solid companies simply caught in the sinking economy along with everything else, then your best course of action may be to sit tight.

Caution ───────────────────────────────────

> Timing is always a critical consideration in asset allocation. Two people
> may approach the same problem with entirely different solutions based
> solely on the difference in time horizons.

I'm a proponent of the buy-and-hold investing philosophy, but a completely passive approach to a recession bear market may be dangerous. If you are approaching your financial goal, staying put may put you at risk of not having time to recover before you need the money.

Remember, bear markets and recessions don't necessarily move in tandem. Consider the frightening prospect of a bear market developing first, followed by a recession. Weakened stocks face an economy that is contracting. Without energy in the economy, how are stocks going to rebound?

A REASONABLE APPROACH

Asset allocation is about planning your participation in the market. That plan needs to include contingencies for dealing with a weakening economy and a bear market to accompany it.

Throughout the rest of this book, we will discuss specific recommendations and ideas about asset allocation for a number of different circumstances. For now, let's stay with the philosophical for a short time more.

Earlier, I said that you could visualize asset allocation as a knob, which you could turn from more to less aggressive (or the other way). It's the same visualization for dealing with a bear market and a recession. You will want to move from a more aggressive stance to a less aggressive stance. If you can do that before the market gets ugly, you will go a long way toward protecting your position.

Tip ───────────────────────────────────

> Actively trading in a nonqualified account may generate more costs in
> commissions and taxes than it saves. Be careful that you don't give all of
> your profits to the government.

If you own primarily individual stocks, realigning your portfolio can be an expensive and a taxing proposition (assuming you are not working in a qualified retirement account).

You may be reluctant to dump depressed but otherwise healthy growth stocks for bonds or cash instruments. The good news is that if you have a relatively well-diversified portfolio with good allocation, you may not have much to do beyond strengthening your conservative side. We will explore specifics in upcoming chapters.

CONCLUSION

Finding what works in a recession bear market is not easy. An aggressive strategy might hurt more than it helps, and a conservative strategy may not help enough.

Common sense may suggest the best strategy is to do nothing. However, given the length of some bear markets that may not be as safe as it may sounds.

CHAPTER 11

ASSET ALLOCATION IN INFLATION AND DEFLATION BEAR MARKETS

Inflation is evil. We all agree on that. Deflation is the opposite of inflation, so deflation must be good, right? Wrong. Deflation is just as evil as inflation, if not more so, but most of us aren't familiar with the evil it can do. Deflation hasn't afflicted the economy in over 70 years, but that doesn't mean it can't come back; in early 2001, several well-respected market commentators began to sound warnings about deflation.

The problem in understanding deflation is that our first reaction is to think it's the opposite of inflation. We think in terms of hot and cold, left and right, up and down, black and white. If you ask 100 people to do a word-association with these terms, almost all of them will give you the second term. Our natural reaction, then, is to think that inflation and deflation are opposites. They are, but they aren't complete opposites—because they both are devastating to the economy.

To understand deflation, we need to get a grip on its definition and what it means in practical terms. I have included both deflation and inflation in the same chapter because it's easier to understand one in the context of the other.

DEFINING INFLATION

When we think of inflation, we see rising prices and interest rates. You often hear inflation discussed in terms of the rising prices of goods. In truth, the value of goods does not rise, but the value of money declines because it takes more money to buy the same item. We talk about interest rates and rising prices, but you don't hear much about the root cause of inflation: too much money chasing too few goods.

Here's a recent example. Before the dot.coms became dot.bombs, housing in Silicon Valley was at a premium. The tremendous growth of Internet/tech companies in the area caused a dramatic rise in housing prices. Houses weren't for sale, they were up for bid—sellers were in the enviable position of having buyers try to outbid one another. It wasn't uncommon for a modest house to sell for several hundred thousand dollars over the asking price.

That's inflation. Too much money chasing too few houses caused a tremendous increase in prices. The house's value continues to skyrocket, and it takes more money to buy it. Inflation causes things, especially hard assets like real estate and gold, to become more valuable than money.

Inflation is great if you are selling real estate, but it's not so great for everyone else. Consider the bank lending money to a customer for a new car. If inflation continues, the money the customer pays back to the bank is worth less than when the bank lent it. The bank attempts to compensate by charging higher interest rates on its loans. That may discourage some buyers from borrowing.

C a u t i o n

> Whether it is real estate, stocks, or Beanie Babies, any item bid up in price beyond a sustainable level is bound to fall eventually.

This is what the Fed does when it raises interest rates to cool rising inflation. Higher rates mean fewer people are borrowing and there is less money chasing goods. Higher interest rates effectively take money out of the market.

DEFINING DEFLATION

If inflation causes the value of money to fall, then deflation should cause the value of money to rise. That doesn't seem like a bad thing, but the result is dramatically falling prices. When there is too little money chasing too many goods, prices drop. Deflation officially occurs when prices fall enough to cause a sustained decline in the Consumer Price Index (CPI)—although some observers believe the CPI is hopelessly flawed and isn't valid as a measure to predict the immediate future. Companies slash prices to move goods, which squeezes profit margins. The more goods a company produces, the worse the situation becomes.

Caution

When our money becomes more valuable, the prices of foreign goods drop dramatically. If they flood the market, domestic competitors may face dramatic reversals.

In a deflation scenario, money increases in value and goods decrease. Consumers want money—or, more precisely, cash—because it will be worth more tomorrow while goods will be worth less. Consumers avoid spending precious cash on depreciating goods. This drives down prices. Businesses find it hard to make a profit, and their stock suffers.

Deflation as an economy-wide event is virtually unknown in modern times. The last time we suffered a serious deflation was in the Depression of the 1930s. When the stock market crashed, 90 percent of its value disappeared in a matter of a few days. All of this wealth simply went away. Cash became the precious resource, and people struggled to get it any way they could. Men selling apples on the street and children selling pencils are some of the enduring images of the Depression.

Tip

Pundits are fond of saying a market crash like the one that preceded the Great Depression can't happen again. However, we have seen several instances where prices have declined dramatically in a short period.

SOME MODERN EXAMPLES

How does all of this relate to the stock market and protecting yourself in unstable times? Depending on whom you talked to in early 2001, a recession combined with inflation or deflation was upon us.

Remember, recession and inflation or deflation are not mutually exclusive. We have had both recessions (and depressions) with either inflation or deflation.

RECENT INFLATION

Earlier I noted that the Fed is not responsible for the stock market. That's true, but it doesn't mean the Fed is unconcerned with the market. During the height of the late-1990s bull market, the Fed raised interest rates six times in order to cool off the economy. The Fed attempted to take money out of the economy by discouraging borrowing.

One factor the Fed considered before raising interest rates was the incredible "wealth effect" created by the exploding Internet/tech stocks. During the last few years of the bull market, companies were issuing IPOs like there was no tomorrow. Companies that a few months earlier had been an idea on a bar napkin suddenly had market caps in the hundreds of millions of dollars. Some soared into the billions of dollars as their stock went from, for example, $25 per share to $125 per share almost overnight. Employees, directors, and investors held options for tens of thousands of shares at pennies per share.

Caution ───────────────────────────────

> Although there has been a tremendous shakeout in the Internet/tech sector stocks, don't dismiss the survivors out of hand. Some of them could be the leaders in the next bull market.

Imagine that one day you're sleeping in your clothes because you've been working around the clock to launch a new Internet product or service, and the next day you're worth $300 million dollars. The company you started has a market cap in the billions of dollars, and it has never generated a nickel of revenue. That's the wealth effect, and it's very inflationary. The people who bid for houses have the wealth effect.

The huge run-up in Internet/tech stocks is a good illustration of inflation. Investors couldn't throw money at the stocks fast enough. Adding new stocks (IPOs) only increased the amount of money flowing into the market. Too much money chasing too few goods: Investors believed the stock would be worth more tomorrow than today.

The Fed's interest-rate hikes aimed in part at taking some of the money out of the market, since many investors were using margin accounts to increase their holdings.

RECENT DEFLATION

Can you see what's coming? When the Nasdaq cratered beginning in March 2000, the Internet "bubble" burst in a rather dramatic fashion. The market lost over 57 percent of its value in one year. For many of the dot.coms it was even worse. Many lost up to 90 percent of their value, and some just disappeared.

When the Nasdaq loses 57 percent of its value, it's a huge sum of money. Where did it go? It vaporized. To get an idea of how much value vaporized, consider the Nasdaq 100 Index, which is 100 of the top Nasdaq stocks. In a one-year period beginning in early 2000, the companies represented in the index lost $2.2 trillion in value (market capitalization).

You could argue that that wasn't "real" money but paper profits that were unrealized. That's not really material to this discussion. The stock had value, and stockholders expressed that value in dollars. When investors challenged that value, they began a panicked retreat from stock to cash. The turn from boom to bust represents a turn from acquiring stock at almost any cost (inflation) to selling stock at any price (deflation).

Tip ———————————————————————————————

> The huge amount of wealth created in the Internet/tech boom was much more than paper profits. If you sold before the bust, you got real money; some employees who held certain classes of options had to pay taxes on them even if they were unexercised.

The Fed lowered interest rates twice in January 2001 with more cuts hinted in the near future. If raising interest rates keeps inflation under control, then lowering rates should check deflation, although no one at the Fed was talking about deflation at the time of the cuts. Lowering interest rates adds money to the economy by making it easier and more cost effective to borrow. Businesses borrow to finance expansion, and consumers borrow to acquire assets such as cars and houses.

It will take more than a few interest-rate cuts to turn around a roaring bear market, but many saw the initial cuts as a positive sign.

WHAT YOU CAN DO WHEN INFLATION HAPPENS

Investors face some tough choices in figuring out what is going on with the economy even in the best of times. Will the market lead the economy or follow it? If inflation causes a bear market, how can you deal with its effect on your portfolio?

Except in extreme cases of inflation and tough bears, there are market assets you can use to help offset the effects of inflation. Large cap stocks normally will outperform inflation. In other words, if inflation is 6 percent, you can expect a greater than 6 percent return from large cap stocks. Of course, not just any large cap stock will do. The company or mutual fund must be growing at a substantial and sustainable rate to overtake and pass inflation. This may be hard in a bear market when investors are discounting certain sectors.

Tip

Whether the government declares the official beginning of inflation or deflation is of little importance. Investors can feel the bad effects of the two conditions without any official declaration.

Unfortunately, even the large cap stocks may not keep up with inflation, which was the case in the late 1970s. The rate of inflation and how quickly it appears also contribute to the success or failure of your strategy. Plan for a long-term return, because in the short-run, few common stocks are going to outperform inflation.

Bonds are particularly at risk in inflation, mainly for the high interest rates and reduced earnings power. The interest rate a bond pays will soon be uncompetitive if newer bonds boast a higher rate.

For example, say you bought a $10,000 bond paying six percent interest at maturity. At maturity, the issuer pays you $10,600. However, inflation was 4 percent for the year; so instead of getting back $10,600, you actually receive $10,176 in purchasing power.

Bond price: $10,000

Interest: $600

Due at maturity: $10,600

Less 4% inflation: ($424)

Value of cash return: $10,176

Buyer's return: 1.76%

Now, suppose you wanted to sell the bond after one year on the open market. Inflation has driven up interest rates and eaten into the return. To sell this bond, you will have to discount it so the buyer's return takes into account the higher interest rates and diminished purchasing power. Instead of selling the bond for $10,000, you can only get $9,000.

Bond price: $9,000

Interest: $600

Due at maturity: $10,600

Less 4% inflation: ($424)

Value of cash return: $10,176

Buyer's return: 11.95%

Discounting the bond's price from $10,000 to $9,000 raises the actual return to 11.95 percent. The amount of loss to inflation is the same for both because it is on the bond's face value and interest. The "value of cash return" is what you receive at the bond's maturity from the issuer, so it remains the same. The buyer's return is what the holder receives less the lost purchasing power from inflation.

Tip

> Gold has been a traditional safe haven from inflation. In the 1970s and
> 1980s, many people bought actual gold bullion or coins. However, don't
> assume that a hard asset like gold or real estate will hold its value when
> inflation subsides—in most cases it won't.

In Chapter 12, "Bear-Proof Assets," we will look at specific tips and tools
for investing during an inflation bear market.

WHAT YOU CAN DO ABOUT DEFLATION

Deflation poses some difficult problems for investors. For one thing, it is
virtually unknown to modern investors. There are no past periods to look
back on for guidance or suggestions.

A bear market caused by deflation would be a particularly tough situation. Falling prices would affect virtually every sector of the economy.
Consumers might be afraid to part with precious cash to buy anything
but the necessities. Businesses would struggle under the weight of reduced
demand and falling prices. Investors should avoid borrowing and investing in common stocks that don't pay dividends. Real estate and other hard
assets like gold will not do well in deflation.

Deflation rewards lenders, since the debtor repays with money that
is worth more than the original note. Fixed-income products and
dividend-paying stocks would do better than other investments.

Caution

> Avoid borrowing during a deflationary period if possible. You will be re-
> paying the debt with money that is worth more than when you bor-
> rowed it.

Bonds would be a logical choice for investors to use as protection against
deflation. In normal markets, long-term bonds are more risky than
short-term instruments because there is a greater chance interest rates
will rise over time. During deflation, however, the interest and principal

you receive at maturity are worth more over time. Let's look at our bond example from the inflation section.

In the deflation scenario, the value of the bond increases, thanks to money buying more than in the past and interest rates falling if you hold it to maturity.

Bond price: $10,000

Interest: $600

Due at maturity: $10,600

Less 4% inflation: ($424)

Value of cash return: $11,024

Buyer's return: 10.24%

Your actual return in terms of buying power is boosted by the 4.24 percent deflation factor (6% + 4.24% = 10.24%). This is a dramatic illustration of the effect deflation would have on the market. Anyone with cash to lend could command the best deals. Obviously, the interest rate on new bonds would drop to something less than 6 percent.

Let's continue our example and look at selling the bond during deflation. The assumption is that you bought this bond in a "normal" market and six percent was a reasonable return. Falling interest rates to combat the deflation raise the value of this bond by increasing its sale price in the secondary market.

Bond price: $10,500

Interest: $600

Due at maturity: $10,600

Less 4% inflation: ($424)

Value of cash return: $11,024

Buyer's return: 4.99%

In this case, the buyer on the secondary market might settle for this interest rate knowing that deflation was adding 4 percent per year to the value of her cash return.

CONCLUSION

Bear markets brought on by either inflation or deflation are devastating to the economy and the stock market. Both represent a weakness in our monetary system. In other countries that have faced these two challenges, economies have crumbled under the distrust this weakness generates.

Distrust in the money system is dangerous. Investors face the quandary of where to put their money so that it is safe. Hoard money during inflation and it will lose its value. Invest your money during deflation and what you buy will be worth less tomorrow than it is today.

In Chapter 12, we are going to look at a number of financial scenarios and examine what products work best in those circumstances.

BEAR-PROOF ASSETS

Investing is about uncertainty. You don't know for sure what the stock market is going to do next year, next month, next week, or even tomorrow. Unless you are 100 percent invested in U.S. Treasury Bonds, there are virtually no guarantees on the future value of your holdings.

Your goal as an investor is to put together a portfolio that offers the best possible return for today's market and tomorrow's uncertainty. This means you need to understand how certain investments normally fare in different market conditions. For example, how will stocks, bonds, and cash react to an expanding market? What can you expect if the market is contracting?

In the interest of full disclosure, the title of this chapter is more marketing than factual. There is no way to completely protect your portfolio from the ravages of a bear market and still stay invested. Hiding places may be hard to find in the midst of a recession marked by high inflation and interest rates. Investors in the "super bear" market of 1973 and 1974 couldn't find a rock big enough to hide under for protection. The best they could hope for was damage control.

This chapter looks at all varieties of investments and how they might fare in a bear market, to help you decide which tools work best for your asset-allocation model. We have seen that bear markets come in several shapes, so what might work in one bear market won't do well in another. A well-diversified portfolio is your best defense.

STOCKS IN A BEAR MARKET

Conventional wisdom says that most stocks will fall in a bear market. This assumes a market-wide bear situation, which occurs less frequently than bear attacks on industry sectors.

Obviously, there is more than one type of stock, just as there is more than one type of bear market. Historically, large cap stocks (generally considered $5 billion and over) have performed better than smaller stocks. Larger companies have more resources to weather bad economic cycles often associated with bear markets. Given the meltdown of more than a few large or near large cap Internet/tech stocks, we should amend the designation to read large, established companies.

Caution ─────────────────────────────

> No company is immune from the ravages of bear markets and economic instability. Some get back on their feet quickly, while others never seem to recover completely.

However, even well-established large companies can suffer hard times, whether in response to a bear market or due to changes in the competitive environment. Three of the leaders in the Internet/tech market boom, Microsoft, Intel, and Cisco Systems, suffered huge stock losses when the dot.com era came crashing down. What happened? How could Microsoft, whose operating system is in 95 percent of the personal computers; Intel, whose chips power most of those computers; and Cisco Systems, whose networking devices were the backbone of the Internet, falter?

There were several reasons, including a general slowing in the economy that indicated slower growth for these growth stocks. The growth of the personal-computer market slowed as fewer people became first-time owners. This meant fewer computers, fewer chips, and fewer fees for software. New producers of networking equipment and computer chips added pressure.

When growth stocks don't grow as fast as the market thinks they should, stock prices fall. Will Microsoft, Intel, and Cisco Systems be around after the bear market disappears? Almost certainly; however, they may not reclaim their place as absolute market leaders.

THE INDUSTRY SECTOR IS IMPORTANT, TOO

It's not enough to know how different types of stocks might act in a bear market. The other important piece of information relates to the company's industry sector. Different sectors handle the causes of bear markets (for example, inflation, recession, deflation, and so on) with various degrees of success.

Later in this chapter, we will look at the main industry sectors and which ones offer possible shelter and which ones to avoid. Let's look at how some different types of stocks might fare in an unstable market.

LARGE CAP STOCKS

Large cap stocks have market capitalizations in excess of $5 billion. Before the Internet/tech bubble, it would take a company many years to achieve this size.

As noted, larger companies typically have the resources to weather bear markets, especially those associated with recessions. Their stocks may be battered, but when the market turns up, they're in a better position to regain lost ground.

> **Plain English**
>
> You compute the **market capitalization** by taking a stock's price and multiplying it by the number of outstanding shares. For example, a company has 1,000,000 shares outstanding and its market price is $100 per share. The market cap is $100 million.

Not all large cap stocks are equal. As we will see in the later discussion of industry sectors, being large is not always a shield against determined bears.

GROWTH STOCKS

Growth stocks are particularly vulnerable during a recession/bear market. The usual reason for investing in a growth stock is to participate in its future growth. When a growth stock quits growing or even slows down, investors may jump ship for other opportunities. A recession or slowing economic growth can hurt most growth companies.

The PC industry was facing this problem even before the Internet/tech bubble burst in the spring of 2000. The computer industry experienced tremendous early growth; however, once the middle- to upper-income market was saturated, growth began to slow. Although prices have dropped dramatically, computers are still a stretch for many households with modest incomes. There is still good volume in replacing older computers, but new growth is getting harder and more expensive (lower prices and margins).

A recession or slowing economic growth gives bears all the incentive they need to look for safer ground. Just as growth stocks may be the first hit in a bear market, they often lead the way out. For this reason, investors must carefully weigh the value of owning the stock through difficult times. When the bulls return, is this stock going to lead the charge? If you believe the company is fundamentally sound, you may want to buy more at a bear market discount. You will learn more about this in Chapter 15, "Fatten Up on Bear."

DIVIDEND-PAYING STOCKS

Companies pay dividends based on the performance of the company, not the stock. Many established large cap stocks pay regular dividends. This income-producing benefit may make them attractive in bear markets. Even if the stock has fallen into a bear-market slump, the company will often continue paying dividends; as a rule, these stocks are less volatile in good times and in bad.

Inflation is not kind to companies paying dividends, since rising prices erode the value of the dividend. On the other hand, deflation makes these stocks especially attractive since the value of money rises in deflation.

VALUE STOCKS

A value stock trades close to its true market value. For example, when some growth stocks are sporting P/E ratios of 35 and above, a value stock might come in with a P/E in the low teens.

By definition, value stocks don't have much of an inflated price and may not move as much as growth stocks in a bear market. Bear markets, however, often create value stocks out of growth stocks. It is likely that in a bear market, you may find some good bargains on stocks that the market has treated badly.

Despite their bad reputation, some of the surviving Internet/ tech stocks have moved into the value category from their once lofty and wildly inflated P/E ratios. Some market watchers were saying in early 2001 that these beaten-up companies deserved a look at their more reasonable valuations.

Tip

Value is in the eye of the beholder. Just because a stock is off by 60 percent doesn't mean it's a bargain. You determine valuation by the company's fundamentals, not by how far it has fallen.

OTHER LARGE CAP STOCKS

Market professionals apply a number of other classifications to stocks, such as "classic growth," "speculative growth," "hybrids," and so on. Rather than going through each one and undoubtedly leaving some out, let's look at the commonsense way to decide if a stock is a bear killer or bear bait.

In broad terms, a bear market usually signals a move by investors from aggressive to conservative. Stated another way, investors look for stability in the midst of uncertainty. Remember, it's not the bear market that cripples a company, but the underlying causes of bear markets such as inflation, deflation, and/or recession. Companies that were speculative before a recession or slowdown may be in serious trouble early in the cycle.

When we look at actual asset-allocation formulas later in the book, the amount of risk (or aggression) you can tolerate will play a large role in devising your plan. Some investors with long time horizons and a high aversion to risk stick with traditional "blue-chip" stocks for security. Investment advisors refer to these stocks (think of the stocks in the Dow) as "widows and orphans." This means these stocks would be suitable for investors with a low tolerance for risk.

Large cap stocks are certainly one class you can look at in the face of a charging bear market. However, if the bears are eyeing industry segments, like when they attacked the Internet/tech segment, you had best get out of their way.

MID CAP GROWTH STOCKS

Mid cap stocks have market capitalizations of $1 to $5 billion. They represent companies that have moved out of a startup mode and into the maturing process. They are also prime candidates for mergers and acquisitions because they have established their business model, technology, and/or market penetration.

A few mid cap stocks will make it into the large cap range, but most will stay at this size if not bought or merged. In general, size plays an important role in determining how risky a stock is relative to industry peers. Mid cap stocks, on this basis, are by definition more risky than large cap stocks.

That statement breaks apart when comparing two companies. There are large cap stocks that are certainly speculative, as there are mid cap stocks on the more conservative side.

Mid cap growth stocks represent an attractive target for investors hoping to spot a new industry leader still in its emerging stage. Mid cap stocks, especially those in a "hot" sector, are prime candidates for spectacular growth. Investors with a moderate tolerance for risk find the stocks appealing because they have moved into a more established posture but haven't nearly exhausted their growth potential.

However, mid cap stocks may be more vulnerable to conditions behind a bear market like inflation, deflation, or recession. The bear market may be particularly cruel to mid cap stocks.

T i p ───────────────────────────────────────

> Mid cap stocks represent a moderately aggressive investment and should occupy that spot in your asset-allocation strategy.

Investors looking for safety and stability often dump mid cap stocks in favor of more secure investments in larger cap stocks or other vehicles, like bonds. However, investors face the same question as holders of large cap growth stocks. Will the underlying causes of the bear market permanently injure the company, or does it have the resources to catch an upturn?

Your personal investment situation and asset-allocation model will help you decide on the risk of riding out a bear market. If you are concerned about an approaching bear market or conditions that suggest a slowdown in the economy, you may want to think carefully about how much of your portfolio is in mid cap stocks.

OTHER MID CAP STOCKS

Other types of mid cap stocks (value, hybrid, speculative growth, and so on) face the same influences as large cap stocks; however, these companies have fewer resources to weather a poor economy.

It's not unusual to see mid cap stocks begin to slide when the market and economy look unstable. Investors know that smaller companies are likely to find continued growth difficult in tough economic times.

Excellent research is important in deciding whether to hold on to a mid cap stock or let it go. You can be certain General Electric is going to survive a recession. However, smaller companies that depend directly or indirectly on consumer demand may find a protracted recession or other economic instability an extraordinary burden.

These companies, assuming they are fundamentally sound, are merger or an acquisition candidates. Stepping under the financial umbrella of a much larger company may give them the breathing room needed to flourish. Mergers and acquisitions under these conditions may not be at any market premium—I wouldn't hold stock in these companies hoping that a merger or an acquisition will be at a large premium.

SMALL CAP STOCKS

Investors should double every concern and warning about mid cap stocks for small cap stocks, which have market caps of $1 billion and under. These small companies are frequently very young and unproven in the marketplace. Their mortality rate is high, especially in technology and other highly competitive industries.

Investors are attracted to small cap stocks because of the tremendous growth potential, but with this potential comes an appropriate amount of risk. Economic downturns can prove disastrous for small cap companies that lack the financial resources to ride out a prolonged period of inflation, deflation, or recession.

However, a slowing economy may not dramatically affect a small company running on cash from a recent IPO. It could be in a great position when the market turns upward again.

Small cap stocks are highly speculative under almost any circumstance. You should carefully evaluate their place in your portfolio relative to your tolerance for risk and time horizon.

FOREIGN STOCKS

It is easier to invest in foreign companies now because more information is available, and most investment professionals believe foreign stocks have a place in every well-diversified portfolio after core investments are in place.

Foreign stocks carry some additional risks, such as political instability, that aren't real factors in domestic stocks. However, foreign stocks may also be a source of strength during a major bear market: Our economic problems may not affect another country. I say "may" because the world economies are more intertwined than ever before, and, as globalization continues, that interdependence will continue to rise.

BONDS

Bonds are traditional core investments used to add stability to the volatility of stocks in portfolio. Bonds are more conservative than stocks because of their fixed return and guaranteed principal in some cases. U.S. Treasury issues are the most secure investment because they are backed by the "full faith and credit" of the U.S. government. Later in the book, when we discuss specific asset-allocation strategies, you will see the key role bonds play in the process.

Tip

> Bonds appear boring to many investors because they lack the sense of urgency stocks have based on how the media reacts. Interestingly enough, there is more money in the bond market than the stock market.

Investors flock to bonds during periods of instability. On most days when the market is down significantly, you will see a rise in the amount of money flowing into the bond market. You normally give up some return for this stability, but not always. The 10-Year Treasuries, which are the bond market's benchmark, gained over 14 percent in 2000, while the S&P 500 lost over 9 percent.

Their predictable returns make bonds a good choice in most situations. One notable exception is during periods of high inflation. The Fed will typically raise interest rates to cool inflation, and bonds react negatively to rising interest rates because their return is fixed. If you can buy a $10,000 bond with an 8 percent interest rate, what would you pay for a similar bond with a 10 percent interest rate?

Caution ──

Bonds are not as easy to research and trade as stocks. If you are going to actively trade bonds, you may want to seek the help of a professional.

The longer term the bond has, the higher the coupon or interest rate will be. This is because, over time, interest rates are likely to rise and force the bondholder to sell at a discount to be competitive. In Chapter 5, "Market Indicators," we discussed the problems with selling bonds in a period of rising interest rates.

You can approach bonds from two directions. First, you can be an active trader, buying and selling them on the open market. In this scenario, the bond's price relates to its coupon interest rate and the prevailing market interest rates for the same type of bond.

Second, you can buy bonds with the notion of holding them until maturity. This takes the fluctuation out of the picture because you are more concerned with receiving your full principal at maturity on a specific date. This strategy is common when investors need a certain sum of money at a specific time (for college tuition, say). When you employ this strategy, you are not concerned with the market fluctuation. Your concern is having money available when you need it.

You are better off establishing a minimum bond presence in your portfolio and adding to it if economic and market conditions call for more protection. When we look at specific strategies later, you will see how timing bonds' maturities can add a new dimension to your portfolio.

MUTUAL FUNDS

Mutual funds, except for sector and other specialized funds, tend to be more stable than individual stocks because of their diversification. The operative word here is diversification, because you can't always assume you are buying a diversified portfolio in a particular mutual fund.

A large cap stock fund loaded with technology stock is not going to perform the same way as a large cap stock fund that truly spreads investments across several industry segments. We have already noted that you can't always judge mutual funds by their names. You should look into Morningstar.com for information about what the fund actually holds, instead of what the name implies.

Index funds, especially those targeting major indexes like the S&P 500, are down in a bear market and back up when the tide turns. They are a way through bear markets with some assurance they will follow the market up.

Bear markets offer an attractive dollar cost–averaging opportunity to the committed index fund investor. If individual stocks post peaks and valleys of performance, diversified stock mutual funds tend to be rolling hills.

BOND FUNDS

Bond funds are popular with investors for many of the same reasons equity funds are popular. They offer professional management and diversification. In the case of bonds, mutual funds are much easier to buy and sell than individual bonds. Bond funds may be an attractive safe haven in bear markets, but if you need a specific sum of money at a specific time, you should consider individual bonds.

Because bond funds buy issues with different maturities, you cannot count on them to return your principal intact on the date you need it.

Tip

> Mutual funds come in many varieties and attempt to address many different investment needs. There is a danger in trying to micro-manage your portfolio by loading up with very specialized funds. Most investment professionals caution that owning too many funds is overkill.

HYBRID FUNDS

Hybrid or balanced funds invest in both stocks and bonds, as well as cash instruments. They spread money across all three areas and move it around as market conditions suggest.

For example, if technology stocks are hot, the fund will move money out of bonds and cash and into hot stocks. Likewise, they may take a more conservative stance if stocks are weak and the market uncertain.

Hybrid funds have differing approaches, so make sure you know what the fund manager's strategy is before you invest. One of the negatives about investing in hybrid funds is they can run up some significant fees and taxes.

BEAR FUNDS

It might not surprise you to know there are mutual funds designed to deal with bear markets. These funds employ a variety of strategies to move in the opposite direction of a bear market. The fund managers use tools like shorting stocks that they believe will decline in a bear market. They may also short index futures and other derivatives. The downside with these funds is they have a bad habit of missing the boat when the market turns upward.

MARKET NEUTRAL FUNDS

Market neutral funds look to hit a target return, no matter what the market is doing at the moment. They invest in undervalued stocks, hoping to ride them up, and short overvalued stocks they believe will fall.

This strategy rests on the managers picking the right stocks, and that is a difficult task under any circumstances.

BEAR RANKING FUNDS

Morningstar.com has a tool that allows you to rank a fund based on how it will likely do in a down market. Although not foolproof, it is a useful screen for narrowing down funds to examine.

You can find the tool under their "Quicktakes" section and rank funds by market volatility. The ranking examines funds for performance during previous downturns. This ranking will tell you how well the fund weathered previous downturns and is a helpful tool. However, like all tools that examine past performance, it can't forecast future performance with certainty; too many variables can change from one down market to the next.

Caution

There are no magic funds that are going to protect you completely from a bear market. Common sense and a well-diversified portfolio are always your best defense.

SECTORS

I'm from Texas, so believe me when I say size matters. However, it is not the only consideration. Industry segment is also important. A company in the "wrong" industry segment or sector is also likely to fall during a bear attack on other members of the segment.

Industry segments such as technology, durable goods, real estate, and so on behave differently in a bear market. The proper mix in your asset-allocation plan is a big step toward bear-proofing your portfolio.

Caution

> Predicting a sector's performance during a bear market is not a sure thing. Underlying economic factors can change predicable behavior.

Investors traditionally look to some sectors for shelter during bear markets and unstable economies. These are general guidelines only; bear attacks can take many forms, and a sector may not always respond the way you think it should. There are many segments, but most market observers cluster them into just a handful for convenience. These include …

- **Consumer durable goods.** This sector includes major appliances and items with an expected life of more than three years. It will suffer in a prolonged recession marked by high interest rates.

- **Nondurable goods (staples).** This sector includes food, clothing, and other items necessary for daily life, which are consumed immediately or have only a short period of usefulness. This has been a favorite hideout because it seldom suffers dramatically in a recession.

- **Energy.** Energy is a very volatile sector, in part because foreign interests exert so much influence over prices, and domestic producers are highly regulated.

- **Industrial cyclicals.** These stocks are not usually a good haven because they flow with the economy. When the economy is down, they will be among the first to fall.

- **Services.** Services have become a huge part of our economy. It's not normally a very volatile sector, but it offers no real protection either.

- **Real estate.** Real estate is extremely interest-rate sensitive, so declining interest rates will spur growth. If the Fed is fighting off a recession or deflation, it will use interest-rate cuts. However, if inflation is the biggest fear, interest rates will rise, and that will slow consumer demand. Commercial real estate thrives in inflationary periods because it increases in value with inflation.

- **Technology.** Technology is no haven from bear markets. An extended downturn in the economy thwarts growth, and that negatively affects technology stocks, which are almost all growth stocks.

- **Financial services.** Financial services are also interest-rate sensitive (if consumers and businesses aren't borrowing, financial companies suffer). There is more to the sector than banks and savings and loans; however, falling interest rates are good news for them all. Watch out for rising rates if the Fed smells inflation.

- **Utilities.** Utilities used to be the favorite hideout for risk-adverse investors. For the most part, they are stable, solid companies that pay handsome dividends. Today, some of these same conservative utilities are venturing into a variety of other businesses (telecommunications, for example). Others are facing deregulation and a variety of new competitors that didn't exist before. If you include the telecoms in this sector (as opposed to technology), you're looking at a group of highly leveraged companies that have expanded at breakneck speed, primarily on debt. Not the safest place to be.

- **Healthcare.** Healthcare firms have ridden the market up and down, but if you're looking for stability, look elsewhere. Rising costs that are outpacing payments put healthcare providers in tough circumstances.

- **Retail sales.** Retail sales are not the place to avoid bad economic news. Even though people still buy items, recessions tend to take the confidence out of buyers.

Caution

Investing in sectors, whether through mutual funds or individual stocks, can be dangerous. That strategy defeats the purpose of diversification. Sector investing is a high-risk maneuver.

Traditional investment thought believes each sector has certain characteristics that suggest how it will react in a bear market. For example, utilities are considered very conservative investments. Many still are, but deregulation and other changes have challenged this broad stroke. Some utilities have diversified out of traditional areas, while others are struggling under massive debt incurred to replace aging facilities.

BEAR ATTACKS

Although bears sometimes attack the whole market, they are often more selective, picking out a particular sector to ravage. The bears attacked the Internet/tech sector in the spring of 2000, which led to a widespread bear attack on most of the market.

Morningstar.com has an interactive chart on the lead page of their stock research. This chart tracks several indicators and one of them is 10 sectors they follow. In March 2001, I set the time frame on the chart for one year and looked at their sectors. Each of them was up, except for technology, which was down 50-plus percent for the 12-month period. This shows how the broad market remained up even though it was declining toward the end of 2000, while technology was in a nosedive.

When I change the time frame to "year-to-date," all of the sectors are down except consumer durables. This indicates a general decline in the market consistent with a broad-based bear attack.

CONCLUSION

Stocks and bonds react differently to a variety of economic and market uncertainties. There is not always a clear strategy that will work every time. It is important to understand the basis for the bear market. Inflation often draws interest rate hikes while deflation and a general economic downturn usually indicate interest-rate cuts are coming.

Certain sectors are safer havens than others are. Your best defense is always a well-diversified portfolio.

PART 4

BEAR TRACKING

Part 4 looks at how investors can devise strategies for making age-appropriate decisions about bear market protection. People are living longer, and some of the old rules about asset allocation haven't kept up with the times.

We will also look at how to deal with the need to park cash or meet short-term goals. A short-time horizon is the riskiest of all investment problems. If you're too conservative, you may not meet your goal; however, if you're too aggressive, the bears may make you sorry.

Bear markets can also be an opportunity to pick up some bargains when the bears hammer basically sound stocks along with everything else. This gets dangerously close to market timing, so beware.

CHAPTER 13

AGE-APPROPRIATE STRATEGIES

As we grow older, our focus and priorities constantly shift. Obviously, a 25-year-old single person has much different needs and concerns than a 55-year-old person with a family to support. What isn't always so obvious is how your asset allocation should shift as you age, to strike the right balance between aggressive and conservative investing.

Your best protection against a bear market and economic uncertainty is a well-thought-out asset-allocation plan. As noted earlier, asset allocation is a dynamic process. Your plan should take into consideration your tolerance for risk, your age, the time horizon, and your main financial goal, and you should review and adjust your allocation periodically. Your time horizon is the number of years until you will need money out of your investments—for example, at retirement. The proximity of your time horizon may have a profound affect on your asset-allocation plan.

In this chapter, we will focus on age-appropriate strategies, which will include components of risk tolerance discussed in earlier chapters, and look at how your plan will shift as your time horizon approaches.

DISPELLING SOME MYTHS

As you begin thinking about protecting yourself from a bear market, you may run into a couple of mythical rules of asset allocation:

- The "100 minus your age" rule
- The "very conservative retiree" rule

These, of course, are "rules of thumb," not hard-and-fast restrictions. For years, financial advisers have used the "100 minus your age" rule to determine how much of your portfolio should be in stocks. Here's how it works: A 55-year-old would have 45 percent of his portfolio in equities, while a 30-year-old would have 70 percent of her portfolio in equities.

The problem with this model? It's too simple. It doesn't take into account a number of variables, all of which we'll discuss in this chapter:

- People are living longer
- Risk tolerance varies from person to person
- Time horizon to financial goal

The second rule suggests that a person approaching retirement should retreat into very conservative investments. Although it's appropriate to back off some aggressive investing patterns as retirement approaches, it's possible to be *too* conservative and risk outliving your money. A person retiring at age 65 could easily live another 15 to 20 years or more. That could be a long retirement to fund, especially considering that the cost of living will continue to rise.

We have seen how bear markets can be vicious and prolonged. Protecting against such an attack becomes more important as we approach major financial goals.

WE'RE NEVER OUT OF THE WOODS

It is no secret that the population of America is getting older. The baby boomers are beginning to think very hard about retirement and how they're going to make it.

The fastest-growing age group in our population is 85 and older. Thanks to medical advances and a relatively healthy environment, we can all expect to live longer than our parents and grandparents. That's a good thing, but it also poses serious investment problems. The biggest problem is how to protect your portfolio from bear markets and economic uncertainty and not run out of money before your hourglass runs out of sand. Bears love old people because they are so vulnerable. Older people don't have the time: the weapon that bears can't defeat.

Some people address this issue by working after retirement. They may take a part-time job or do consulting work to keep some cash coming in. This extra income supplements retirement benefits and may mean they don't have to reach into the principal as quickly. A second group of retirees has moved past the age when work is an option. They are living exclusively on retirement benefits, such as a pension and Social Security. Both groups have concerns about their retirement portfolio, however they address them.

On the other end of the spectrum are young people just getting started in their careers. They may be married or will be shortly. Retirement is many years away. They're more concerned with building a family, buying a house, and all the other trappings of adulthood.

Bears love young people because they can be too aggressive on short-term goals and step in a bear trap just before they need the money for a down payment.

STRATEGIES THROUGH THE AGES

Now that we have bracketed the age question, let's look at specific age groups and some strategies for avoiding bear bites. The following are good starting points for you to examine and modify to fit your personal situation.

First, some of the logic behind the plans. I have built in some general assumptions for all categories:

* You have a moderate tolerance for risk.

* You are market-neutral, meaning you are neither overly optimistic nor pessimistic about the direction of the market in the near future.

* You're about average in terms of net worth and annual income for your age group.

* These strategies are for long-term and major goals; I discuss short-term strategies in Chapter 14, "Short-Term and Mid-Term Strategies."

- Each age group has four models: three for your investment portfolio and the other for your retirement portfolio, which will be conservative by definition.
- The assets are heavily weighted toward mutual funds because I believe most people don't have the time, patience, or interest to buy individual stocks. If you would rather buy individual stocks, use the fund definitions to guide you toward the correct equities.
- I include a cash component, which can be a money market account, money market mutual fund, bank certificate of deposit, or other instrument.

You can "tune" the plans to be more or less aggressive to your own tastes. The age groupings are arbitrary; feel free to judge whether you belong in a higher or lower group depending on your own situation. As we work through the age groups, I will include any additional information that is particular to that group but may not apply to all age groups.

This is not an exact science and is subject to much interpretation. Any two financial advisers might suggest two different plans. Some advisers don't include a cash component, but I believe people tend to ignore the need for emergency cash unless you build it into an overall plan.

AGES TWENTY TO THIRTY

This age group is transitioning from young person to young adult. You are into your first or second real job and are beginning to build a nest and acquire the trappings of adulthood. There are two important decisions you need to make immediately:

- A commitment to fund your retirement from day one on the job
- A commitment to pay yourself first through an automatic investing program

These decisions will build habits that, if you stick to them, will almost guarantee you a nice retirement nest egg and an embarrassingly high net worth before you reach age 50.

If your employer offers a 401(k) or other similar retirement program, commit to participating at the maximum or as close to it as possible. If your employer has a matching program, absolutely participate in the plan to the limit of the matching dollars. This is the best investment deal you will ever find that doesn't involve the risk of jail time.

At the same time, begin an investment program that automatically deducts a specific amount from your checking account every month and invests it in a mutual fund. Put $50 a month into a mutual fund and in 30 years you will have over $140,000 (before taxes and assuming the 11 percent historical rate of return by the market). The best part of this is if you start now, you will never miss the money out of your budget. Every time you get a raise, bonus, tax refund, or other income boost, put all or part of it in your investment account.

At this age, you really don't have to worry too much about bear markets. You have plenty of time to recover from any downturns. However, you may want to consider some protection if market or economic conditions look threatening.

Here are some models to fit different investors. Obviously, if you're just getting started, it will take a while to put this mix together. However, if you start early, you could have a large investment and considerably more in your retirement fund. If your employer does not offer a 401(k) or similar program, start an IRA fund and put some extra in your investment account. Remember, these are just to get you started and are not written in stone.

The four models suggest a way to allocate your assets based on how conservative or aggressive (risk-tolerant) you are in investing.

Assets	Regular	Conservative	Aggressive	Retirement
Growth fund		20%	15%	30%
Index funds	25%	35%	15%	50%
Aggressive growth fund	50%		40%	20%
Stocks	15%		25%	
Cash	10%	15%	5%	
Short-term bonds		30%		
Medium-term bonds				
Long-term bonds				
Total:	100%	100%	100%	100%

The Regular model shows your assets spread over several instruments with varying degrees of aggressiveness. The idea is to balance your portfolio with holdings in different asset classes. This is a modestly aggressive model, appropriate for a young adult with many years of investing to come.

The Conservative model drops the two most aggressive assets, the aggressive growth fund and individual stocks, in favor of more money in cash and a significant investment in short-term bonds. This is a very conservative model for a young person, but if it helps you sleep at night, it's worth it. The downside is that if inflation returns with higher interest rates, the bonds will suffer.

The Aggressive model puts 65 percent of its assets into the aggressive growth fund and individual stocks. You could argue that this model doesn't go far enough in its aggressiveness. The downside is obvious: A bear market will eat this portfolio alive.

The Retirement model splits between growth (the aggressive growth fund and growth fund) and a market-following index fund. Some would consider this model too conservative for a young person. It is also unlikely a person in this age range invests just for retirement, but I included it to give you an idea of how a retirement account might be allocated separate from other investments.

AGES THIRTY TO FORTY

Many people in this age range are beginning to advance in their career. They may have a family to support, and their income is increasing. They may be facing some serious financial goals such as home ownership, beginning a college fund, and so on.

Their investment needs are not very different from the previous group, but their total investments may be reaching the point where some protection from bear markets is appropriate.

Assets	Regular	Conservative	Aggressive	Retirement
Growth fund	15%	20%		30%
Index funds	25%	35%	20%	20%
Aggressive growth fund	25%		40%	30%
Stocks	15%		25%	
Cash	5%	10%		
Short-term bonds		35%		
Medium-term bonds	15%			20%
Long-term bonds			15%	
Total:	100%	100%	100%	100%

The Regular model for this age group spreads out the portfolio over more assets and is more conservative than the 20 to 30 Regular model. I added a growth fund and reduced the aggressive growth fund percentage. Stocks remain the same, but I reduced the cash to reflect a more appropriate percentage of the overall portfolio, which should be quite a bit larger than the previous age group's total. I have added medium-term bonds, which are moderately aggressive and may take advantage of falling or stable interest rates.

The Conservative model remains unchanged from the previous age group. It still reflects the position that a bear market will damage your growth fund more than the market as a whole. Leaving the growth fund in the portfolio gives you some upside over the index fund in the event the bear is weak or doesn't appear at all.

The Aggressive model reflects a slightly less robust stance by increasing the participation in the index fund and adding long-term bonds to the mix. The long-term bonds are fairly aggressive—and volatile—in an environment of changing interest rates. I have eliminated cash from the portfolio on the theory that you can put it to better use in an aggressive portfolio.

The Retirement model remains conservative; however, I have dropped the percentage in the aggressive growth fund and added medium-term bonds for some diversification.

AGES FORTY TO FIFTY

You are entering your years of increasing income and responsibilities at work and at home—which is good, because the financial pressures are beginning to bear (there's that pun again) down. Your investment and retirement portfolios may be getting impressive by now if you haven't been ravaged by a bear market. If you've taken a hit, there's still time to recover, but your portfolio should probably be getting more conservative than previous age groups.

Assets	Regular	Conservative	Aggressive	Retirement
Growth fund	20%	20%		30%
Index funds	30%	35%	25%	20%
Aggressive growth fund	20%		35%	20%
Stocks	15%		25%	
Cash	5%	5%		
Short-term bonds		40%		15%
Medium-term bonds	10%		15%	15%
Long-term bonds				
Total:	100%	100%	100%	100%

Our Regular model shows a modest shift toward a more conservative posture. The aggressive growth fund drops and the growth and index funds increase. I have also increased the medium-term bond percentage. This portfolio still represents a diversified look at the market but is moving away from the most aggressive assets and toward those more associated with the center.

This Conservative model shifts money out of cash and into short-term bonds. It retains the percentages in the growth and index funds. To make this model even more conservative, shift more out of the growth fund and into short-term bonds.

This Aggressive model reflects the need to back off slightly as you get older. Some might argue that it is still too soon for conservative measures, but use your own judgment based on your tolerance for risk. This model differs from the previous age group in that the index fund participation increases slightly, the aggressive growth fund decreases slightly, and it moves from the long-term bonds to medium-term bonds.

Our Retirement model continues to move away from the aggressive growth fund and increases participation in the short-term and medium-term bonds. We still have some upside potential with the growth and index funds, while stabilizing the downside with a greater percentage in bonds.

AGES FIFTY TO SIXTY

This is when most of us get serious about retirement—despite my recommendation that you get serious at a young age. You're probably at the peak of your earning power. You may have kids in college or nearly there. You still have a mortgage and other expenses, but retirement is beginning to seem very real.

This is when financial experts advise caution, but there is a danger of being overly cautious and missing out on needed growth. Your portfolio is at its largest, and any compounding will produce some significant increases.

I have added a new asset for this stage, a stock income fund, which reflects the need for reasonably predictable income in your retirement account.

Assets	Regular	Conservative	Aggressive	Retirement
Stock income fund				20%
Growth fund	20%	15%		20%
Index funds	30%	25%	25%	20%
Aggressive growth fund	10%		25%	
Stocks	10%		20%	
Cash	5%	5%		
Short-term bonds	15%	55%		25%
Medium-term bonds	10%		30%	15%
Long-term bonds				
Total:	100%	100%	100%	100%

This Regular model reduces your participation in the aggressive growth fund and stocks, while increasing your exposure in bonds by adding short-term bonds to the mix. You are still 70 percent invested in equities, which may seem high to some; make an adjustment if you feel this is too aggressive for your risk-tolerance level.

This Conservative model shows a strong move away from equities and into bonds. With 40 percent invested in equities, the portfolio still has some room for growth, but it's taking root in bonds for stability and principal protection.

This Aggressive model keeps you in 70 percent aggressive equities (contrast with the Regular model where the equity investments are much more conservative). A 30 percent stake in medium-term bonds provides some stability, although bonds in this maturity range can be volatile.

This mix for a Retirement fund may surprise some of you who question 60 percent in equities. However, if you have a normal life span, you'll have another 20 to 30 years of living to finance. The bond investments should provide some stability and, along with the stock income fund, some current income for reinvestment. The idea here is to build a position in income-producing assets to help with post-retirement expenses.

AGES SIXTY TO SEVENTY

Retirement is at hand! I hope you prepared for it, because it's tough to start now. Many people try to get their financial house in order so retirement is less stressful. A good place to start is to look at any outstanding large obligations. What can you do to get them off your plate? Are you holding any assets in your investment portfolio with losses? If so, now might be a good time to cash them in and take a tax loss. Use the proceeds to pay down or off any major debts.

On or about your sixtieth birthday, you need to figure out what you need to live on after retirement, even if you plan to work. If you have a defined benefits plan (pension) instead of a 401(k) or similar retirement plan, visit your pension representative and discuss how much you can expect.

No matter what kind of retirement plan you have, you will soon be facing some major decisions about its distribution. Tax laws are constantly changing, so talk to an expert in this area to devise a plan.

You are entering a period when you are most vulnerable to a bear attack. Don't be too cautious; however, remember that you may have to finance 20 more years of living.

Assets	Regular	Conservative	Aggressive	Retirement
Stock income fund				20%
Growth fund	30%	15%	25%	20%
Index funds	30%	15%	25%	20%
Aggressive growth fund				
Stocks			20%	
Cash	5%	5%		
Short-term bonds	25%	65%		40%
Medium-term bonds	10%		30%	
Long-term bonds				
Total:	100%	100%	100%	100%

This Regular investment model takes a defensive stance as you enter the years just preceding your retirement. You have reduced your exposure to 60 percent equities. Your position in bonds is now 35 percent. If you are nervous about this model's aggressiveness, reduce your equities and add the percentage into bonds.

Your Conservative model continues a shift out of equities and into bonds. Bonds provide a stability that may be reassuring at this point in life and probably offer the best protection against a bear market.

This Aggressive model takes you out of the aggressive growth fund and moves you into a regular growth fund. Even though you still may want to be in the market, it's time to take your foot off the gas. You're still 70 percent invested in equities, but they're more conservative than previous age groups.

How you configure your Retirement fund will depend on when and how much you withdraw. This is one suggestion that keeps you in the stock market.

This is such a complicated area. You will do yourself a great favor by hiring a professional to construct a plan for withdrawing money from your various accounts. I suggest a fee-based financial planner who specializes in retirement, or a CPA.

AGE SEVENTY-PLUS

From this age on, generalized plans are meaningless. If you haven't sought professional counsel before now, please do so soon. There's no room for error at this point. A bear market could mean the difference between the retirement you dreamed of and the retirement from hell.

You worked hard all your life and deserve the best in retirement. Don't let a last-minute bear spoil your "golden years."

CONCLUSION

Constructing model investment and retirement portfolios is an exercise in suggestions. Temper these suggestions by your tolerance for risk and willingness to monitor your assets.

Five financial professionals can look at the same individual and construct five different plans to protect his or her portfolio from bear markets. None of them will be necessarily right or wrong, and none of them can guarantee how they will do in a real bear market. However, if you don't make some plans, the bears will eat you alive.

CHAPTER 14

SHORT-TERM AND MID-TERM STRATEGIES

A mid-term financial goal, about 5 to 15 years out, is the most dangerous kind for an investor. You may be saving for college or a down payment on a house, or you may be nearing the end of a longer process, such as retirement. Short-term goals (one to five years) can be even more dangerous if you rely on the market to meet your needs. A bear can jump out of the bushes and attack before you know what happened, leaving you without enough time to recover.

Here is a real-world example: A nonprofit group received a gift from the estate of a supporter. The board of directors decided to use the money to endow a program and placed the money in a mutual fund. The program could operate from the conservative estimate of investment income and the principal would remain intact.

All went well the first year, when the market was healthy, but in the second year, the board was shocked to learn the principal had negative growth in a very down market. (Managers use the term "negative growth" instead of "we lost our shirts.") The situation forced the board to raise additional money to continue the program. The moral: If you need a certain sum of money relatively soon, look for alternatives that bears can't chew.

In Chapter 1, "Bear Markets," we looked at historical bear markets and how long they lasted. There is no rule or guideline for how long bears live; however, we know it can run into the months and years.

SHORT-TERM GOALS: TROUBLE AHEAD

Bears find short-term goals particularly attractive because investors don't have time to recover. You need a strategy that will help you reach your goal and protect the account from a bear market.

You may find yourself in one of two situations:

- You have the money already, and you need someplace out of harm's way to protect it.
- You don't have the full sum and need to continue investing to reach the short-term goal.

The first situation is the easiest since you don't need to earn any more to reach your goal. You need a safe place to put the money for a short time. The second poses a more serious problem: How do you keep building toward your goal and still have some assurance that a bear market isn't going to eat your earnings and then some?

Protecting a short-term position is very important. There are numerous examples, including the one at the beginning of this chapter, of why you can't afford to take chances with a short-term goal. Never take for granted that past performance is any indicator of future returns. Things change and you have to stay informed. You can better meet a precise financial goal in a short period with a fixed-return instrument.

There is nothing worse than finding out the $20,000 you put into the market for your daughter's college tuition is now $16,000. Unfortunately, if you were in the market around the middle of March 2001, that fund might be even less. You need $20,000 in one year. Where do you park your money so that you know the full $20,000 will be there? There are some fairly obvious answers, any of which will work for the short term:

- Bank CDs
- Money market accounts
- Bonds

But the nonprofit organization in the example at the beginning of this chapter needed a certain sum returned from the investment to fund their program. How do you guarantee a specific amount of income from your investment? The safest way is to use one of the instruments just described, with the possible exception of the money market account. You can buy both CDs and bonds with fixed maturities and interest to match your needs.

This strategy is simple and straightforward. Best of all, it's all done with instruments bears can't touch. The downside is that if you need the same amount of return each year, you may find inflation is reducing the value of your principal and its income. At some point, the bond or CD will mature, and you will need to reinvest the principal. You may not be able to get the rate you need in the future. Another problem is CDs lock up your money. If you need it before maturity, it will likely cost you a penalty. The market may discount bonds sold before maturity if interest rates rise.

Still, holding CDs and bonds to maturity ensures that the money will be there when you need it. Sometimes, safety is more important than growth. Don't get greedy with money you know you will need.

T i p

> Safety and a high rate of return are mutually exclusive. If you want a high degree of safety, you must settle for lower returns.

Reaching a short-term goal (fewer than five years) is often more an exercise in saving than investing. In any given short period, you face a real danger of a bear market or major correction.

A number of sites on the Internet offer calculators to help you determine the best path to reach your goal. For example, if you want to save $6,000 in two years, a calculator at Bankrate.com shows you that at 5 percent interest, you need to deposit $242.96 a month. If you can find a safe savings instrument that pays more than 5 percent, the calculator will recalculate your needed deposit.

MID-TERM GOALS: NOW COMES THE HARD PART

Mid-term goals (5 to 10 years) present a special problem. The window of 10 years is more than wide enough to let a bear in, and if that happens, you'll have a hard time meeting the goal. You could use the plans I described in the previous section, but mid-term goals may be too long for saving to be efficient. Besides, a long-term goal nearing its end becomes a mid-term goal by definition. If you are in your 50s, you have a mid-term goal to reach your retirement target.

In the last chapter, we talked about asset allocation in the context of age groups. However, you don't have to be in a particular age group to use the asset allocation models for the later age groups. For example, if you have an eight-year-old child and want to provide $15,000 for her college education, you need to set a target and devise a plan to meet the goal while protecting yourself from bears.

This problem is going to involve some work to solve. A basic investment problem has four variables:

- Amount of time available
- Amount of money available to invest
- Rate of return
- Your tolerance for risk

In our situation, we can't alter the amount of time in the problem; in fact, time will be working against us. The amount of money for investment usually has some practical limits based on the priority of the problem. The rate of return is what we can get from various instruments and is subject to change beyond our control. Your tolerance for risk and common sense will prevent you from attempting an exotic solution.

There are three basic ways to accomplish this goal. (The following examples ignore taxes, fees, and inflation. Obviously, in real life you can't ignore them, but for this exercise let's put them aside for the sake of simplicity. We will also ignore solutions such as home equity loans or other types of borrowing.)

- **Use a savings account that pays 5 percent interest and make monthly deposits.** This method has the most chance for success.

Bear markets don't affect it, and 5 percent is a reasonable savings rate. Unfortunately, it is also the most expensive: To hit your goal of $15,000 in 10 years, you need to deposit $96.60 each month. By the time you reach the $15,000 goal, you've put in almost $11,600. Your money isn't working very hard for you

- **Use a mutual fund that pays 11 percent and make monthly deposits.** The likelihood of this strategy's success is questionable. Finding a mutual fund that pays 11 percent for 10 consecutive years seems unlikely, but for discussion's sake, let's assume one is available. To reach $15,000 in 10 years at 11 percent, you need to deposit $69.13 each month for a total of almost $8,300. This is much more efficient than the savings account.

- **Deposit a lump sum in a mutual fund that pays 11 percent.** To reach your goal of $15,000 in 10 years, you need to deposit $5,000 in the account. At the end of the 10-year period, you would be at your $15,000 goal. This is obviously the most efficient, but it's also the most risky.

T i p

Putting money in a savings account may run counter to all you know about investing, but some place a higher value on the certainty of savings accounts than on the need to achieve the maximum return. There's nothing wrong with using a savings account when you do so as a conscious choice.

You have to navigate a 10-year period without a major setback to meet your goal. Of these three plans, the first one, employing a simple savings account, has the most chance for success. It doesn't worry about bear markets, and a 5 percent interest rate should not be a problem.

The other two plans rely on a mutual fund (or any other investment) returning 11 percent each year for 10 years. It certainly has happened, but I wouldn't bet my daughter's college education on escaping a bear market for that long.

You could look at some other possible investments such as junk bonds, but they're even more unpredictable than mutual funds and stocks. There are also all types of exotic options/futures trading plans. None of these is suitable for the average investor, and most of them lose money anyway.

So, a savings account will get us there, but it will cost the most. Investing for 10 years is the least expensive way to reach our goal, but making it without a downturn seems improbable. Here are the parameters of the problem:

	Savings	**Mutual Fund**	**Lump Sum**
Cost:	$11,600	$8,300	$5,000
Chance of success:	Good	Questionable	Questionable
Chance of bear attack	None	Good	Good

Tip

> Even in bear markets, the Internet overflows with get-rich-quick schemes. Some are complicated hedging plans that the vast majority of investors should avoid. Others are outright frauds. Don't let a bear market frighten you into trying one of these quick fixes to recoup losses.

SOLUTION A: SAVINGS PLAN

The savings plan works, and only hinges on you finding a savings instrument that pays five percent interest. In the event you cannot find a 5 percent return, you'll have to add more money into the monthly deposit.

The calculator on Bankrate.com lets you put in a starting balance. If that 5 percent isn't available, plug your current balance into the calculator, and recalculate the number of remaining months and the interest rate you can secure. The calculator will refigure your monthly deposit with the new information. For example, say you were able to earn the 5 percent interest for 36 months, but you could only find a 4 percent rate after that.

Current earnings: $96.60 per month at 5 percent interest for 36 months = $3,759.17.

To reach your $15,000 goal, you will need to increase your monthly deposit for the remaining seven years to $103.65 at 4 percent interest.

Nothing hard about this solution (if you have the money), and it still keeps the bears off your back.

SOLUTION B: MUTUAL FUND—MONTHLY DEPOSITS

This solution works just like the preceding one with the exception that you face more frequent changes in the rate of return.

Assuming you can start in a normal market, what type of mutual fund should you use? This is more a question about your investing style than finding one correct fund to use. In normal markets, several fund types will get your 11 percent return (and we are assuming it pays a constant 11 percent for the period, which, like I said earlier, is unlikely).

One consideration is an S&P 500 index fund. These funds typically have very low costs and little in the way of tax implications. These funds mimic the market index. The S&P 500 is a very broad look at the market and is not subject to the wild gyrations you see in other indexes. During market volatility, it will not normally decline as fast or go up as fast as some of the other indexes (the Nasdaq Composite, for example). Review the observations in Chapter 12, "Bear-Proof Assets," on how different products react in different market conditions for hints on which funds to select.

If you find yourself in a bull market, index funds do quite well. The Vanguard 500 Index (VFINX) had a spectacular run during the late 1990s bull market before falling into negative numbers in 2000. Catch an express train like this bull market, and you will have your $15,000 in fewer than 10 years.

However, if you are starting in a bear market or one is looming, you need a different strategy. You may want to avoid the market completely until things settle down—in which case, fall back on the previous savings plan.

Don't try to pick the bottom of the market and jump in for the upturn. As we have noted earlier, bear markets are notorious for sending out false signals about rallies. As the Nasdaq Composite began its death spiral in March 2000, where would you have called the bottom? As I am writing this one year later, the Nasdaq is below 2,000. It has lost over

3,000 points in one year. At every mark along the way, some pundit called it the bottom. If anyone says, "It just can't fall any lower," you know differently. Wait until you feel sure the market is on solid ground before transferring out of savings and into a mutual fund.

Use the Bankrate.com calculator to recalculate your monthly deposits after transferring your earnings from savings. At a constant interest rate, the calculator will give you a new monthly deposit number. Unless there is a major change in market conditions, I would monitor the fund weekly and make adjustments quarterly. This is a lot of work, but you can't leave the success of this investment to chance. Ten years from now, you'll have to write a tuition check, and you need to be sure the money is there.

SOLUTION C: MUTUAL FUND—LUMP SUM

If you have a lump sum ($5,000 in this example) to invest now, you may have an easy solution to the problem. As we have seen, this sum will get you to your goal with an 11 percent annual return. However, if you wanted to start this solution in March 2001, it would have been hard to find a fund with a positive rate of return near what you need.

This solution is much like the one above. However, with a lump sum you have some other safe options. Bonds, for example, don't necessarily lock you in until maturity, but you can't be certain what they'll sell for on the open market in the future. If interest rates rise, you'll likely have to discount the bond to match the yield of newer bonds. Bear markets accompanied by inflation won't be kind to bonds. On the other hand, a bear market during a recession may raise the rate of return on bonds, as companies have to pay more for debt in uncertain times.

Tip

Bonds can be a great spot for bear-shy investors if you are avoiding the right kind of bear. However, understanding the bond market is not easy, and you should consider using a professional.

Bond mutual funds are not good choices for short-term investing any more than stock funds are. Once the market turns in your favor, you may want to consider putting the money in over several periods, rather than dumping it in all at once. This takes advantage of the power of dollar cost averaging and may give you a better overall yield.

CONCLUSION

Financial goals that fall into the under-10-year range are particularly perilous for investors. History suggests you can expect at least one bear market in this period, plus several major corrections.

If you need a specific amount of money by a certain date, you have to protect it from bear markets. As we saw in Chapter 1, bear markets can last for months, even years. The recovery usually takes even longer.

Important financial goals demand that you focus on safety as well as growth.

CHAPTER 15

FATTEN UP ON BEAR

Bear markets don't mean that you can't look for profits in the market. They simply mean that you have to look in different places.

Bears are indiscriminate in their attacks—they take down healthy stocks along with weak or obese ones, although the healthy ones *will* bounce back eventually. If you're interested in adding to your portfolio, there just might be some bargains.

However, you need to be very clear on one thing: Just because a stock is down 75 percent doesn't mean it's a bargain—or that it isn't going to fall another 15 percent.

IDENTIFYING BARGAIN STOCKS

If you can't explain in concrete terms why a stock is a bargain, it probably isn't one. Investors who just look at the percentage decline in the stock's price aren't asking the big question: What is this stock *worth*—not what was it selling for in a hyper-bull market?

You answer that question by doing your homework and thoroughly analyzing the business behind the stock. Ultimately, the soundness of the business creates the perception of value in the stock.

Caution

A stock that has fallen by 75 percent is not necessarily a bargain. Some stocks do fall to virtually zero in value. If you don't believe this can happen, ask some of the folks holding stock in the "dot.bombs."

LOOK FOR SIGNS

Bears sometimes attack the whole market and other times individual sectors. The demise of the longest bull market in history began in April 2000, when bears began their sustained attack on Internet/technology stocks. Like most bears, this one threw off confusing signals. Beleaguered investors saw every brief rally on the way down as a sign that a firm bottom was in place. Unfortunately, it wasn't.

When a sector is under attack, few stocks escape. Everything suffers, whether it was really bear food or not. The whole sector may be under attack, but you are interested in one or a small group of stocks you think are ultimately sound. Stocks in a sector can ride a bull up with the same ease that they rode the bear down.

XYZ is a great company with innovative products and a potential market leader in its sector at some time in the future. Right now, its stock is enjoying a dizzying ride upon the back of a bull. Watch XYZ's fundamentals on the way down. Are analysts cutting back on earnings projections? Has the company missed any earnings estimates? After you do your research, you believe XYZ is worth about $20 per share, even though it currently trades at $50 per share.

Caution

You can be your own worst advisor. You convince yourself a stock is going nowhere but up, so you buy at any price. When it starts to fall, you tell yourself it will surely rebound. When it doesn't rebound, you sell at the bottom. Don't feel bad—professionals do the same thing sometimes.

The mistake many investors make is to buy the stock on the way up and sell when it has lost most of its value. If you stick to your analysis, the stock isn't a buy candidate until it reaches the approximate dollar figure it is worth. Don't be dismayed if the stock falls even past the price you set as reasonable. There's nothing reasonable about a bear market.

TROUBLE BY ASSOCIATION

Sometimes the only thing wrong with a stock is the company it keeps. This is especially true when bears are ravaging a market sector. If it even smells like the sector, the stock may come under attack.

A sound company that has its stock beaten up because it is in the wrong sector is an excellent candidate for bargain hunters. When the market begins its upturn, this company is likely to draw much attention from investors looking for a solid buy.

DON'T GIVE YOUR HEART AWAY

Bears love lovers of particular stocks. They know if you fall in love with a stock, you will pay an outrageous price and then hold on until the stock has betrayed you a dozen times and trades at 10 percent of what you paid. You will sell in disgust, and the bear wins again.

Always make the stock come to your price. If it doesn't, move on to something else. There are well over 8,000 individual stocks; surely one of them will catch your eye.

STAYING POWER

The bursting Internet/tech stock bubble taught many investors that just because a company can raise hundreds of millions of dollars doesn't guarantee it will be around in three months. However, there are many companies—some old, some new—that dominate their markets in a way that assures continuance for at least the immediate future.

Microsoft, whether you love it or hate it, isn't going anywhere soon. Microsoft software is in 95 percent of the personal computers in the world, and it will stay there until something cataclysmic happens. Will Microsoft stock return to its previous levels during the raging bull market? What is a reasonable price for the stock? After the 2000–2001 meltdown, the market may have fairly priced the stock for the first time in years.

Make the buy decision based on the fundamentals of the business and what you expect from the stock. A bear market can take the hype out of a stock's price and make it a good buy.

NOTHING LASTS FOREVER

The last section notwithstanding, just because a company has been dominant in the past is no guarantee it will remain so in the future. U.S. Steel was once a symbol of America's industrial prowess. Montgomery Ward was a retailing powerhouse. Apple Computer held the personal computer market in its hand and let it slip away.

The list goes on and on. Once proud leaders—dissolved, bankrupt, or buried by competitors—remind us that companies that fail to evolve and adapt to change are fodder for the scrap heap.

Blue-chip stocks are not immune to bear attacks, and past glories mean nothing to today's investors. It isn't hard to spot companies clinging to outdated business models and pre-Internet strategies. The business press does a good job of pointing out these companies to the public.

A ROSE BY ANY OTHER NAME

In addition to studying a company's fundamentals and market position, you need to anticipate how other investors will view the stock during a rising market. A stock's price is driven up or down by investor demand. If there are more sellers than buyers, the stock's price will fall no matter what the fundamentals look like.

Fundamentals may influence investor demand, but emotions can be even more powerful. The truth of that statement is borne out by the recently burst Internet/tech stock bubble, where fundamentals were nonexistent or ignored. The same emotions that inflated the bubble punctured it. Will other investors see the same rose among the thorns you see? If not, the stock isn't going anywhere.

WHAT DO THE ANALYSTS SAY?

Stock analysts for major investment companies follow stocks and report on them. One of their key tools is estimating future earnings.

Much of this information is available free on the Internet at such sites as Morningstar.com and MSN MoneyCentral.com. Major companies may have a significant number of analysts studying the company and making projections. Projections are very subjective because they call for an interpretation of future events. It's common for two analysts to have very different views on the same company.

One way you can tell if a stock could drop further is to look at the earnings projections from different analysts. If you see a big gap in the estimates, it's a sure sign the stock has not finished its drop in a bear market. Analysts also issue recommendations about whether investors should buy, hold, or sell a stock. There are variations, but the idea is that a stock that analysts move from "buy" to "hold" is going to drop.

> **Tip**
>
> The Internet has done wonders to level the playing field for small individual investors, but it's just a matter of following the money to realize that big institutional investors and wealthy individual investors still get the best information first.

If more analysts are rating a stock a "buy" than one month ago, you can also expect a price increase. Likewise, if more analysts are downgrading from a "buy" to a "hold," expect further price drops.

DEAD-CAT BOUNCE

A "dead-cat bounce" is one of the false signals bears leave. (Please, no angry letters from cat lovers—I don't write the news, I just report it.) This indelicately phrased phenomenon occurs when a stock has fallen from a dizzying height, hits bottom, and briefly rallies.

True believers in the stock will see this as a sign of a return to new heights. Unfortunately, what happens next is not a rally but a continued slide into the dumps. "Dead-cat" stock doesn't rebound or stage a sustained rally. If you're in love with one of these unfortunate stocks, your hopes for a life together are shattered.

A COMPANY IS NOT ITS STOCK

One company's stock sells for $125 per share, while another company's stock sells for $15 per share. If you asked a group of nonprofessional investors which company was better, many would pick the $125 per share company. As consumers from birth, we learn that an item's quality relates directly to its price. High-priced items are high-quality items.

But the Internet/tech stock collapse in the spring of 2000 proved that the quality of a company doesn't directly drive the stock's price. A company's fundamentals certainly influence investors, but the price of a stock is ultimately set in the market where many other forces come to bear (there's that pun again).

Tip

> A company's stock price may or may not be an accurate reflection of the company's value. Stock prices move based on expectations of future events and whether more investors are positive or negative in those expectations.

Bulls are as indiscriminate as bears. When the market is super-heated, as it was in the late 1990s, you find stocks trading in triple digits that weren't worth a single-digit price. Internet/tech companies believed they had to grow very fast to survive and burned through cash like there was no tomorrow—and for many, there wasn't.

Don't confuse a company with its stock price. Bad companies can have very high-priced stock, and good companies can have lower-priced stock. When the bubble bursts and the market clears its collective head, companies with good fundamentals will be popular again. Investors still smarting from high-priced failure will look for solid investments when the market begins a recovery.

PROTECTING YOURSELF

As noted earlier, bears are notorious for sending out false signals. Stocks may rally in what appears to be the end of a bear market, only to fall back even further.

If you think you've found a real bargain, keep the bears from turning around and biting you by using limit sell orders. These orders become market orders if the stock's price falls back to a certain price.

This way of protecting yourself from a stock retreating after a rally works best for stocks you're not interested in holding for a long time, since a volatile stock may drop back far enough to trip the limit sell order.

SHORT-TERM PROFITS

While this borders on speculation, there's no reason not to take advantage of a relatively quick profit when you see one.

The stock market is self-correcting which is why there are bull markets and bear markets. Bears often overcorrect the market, especially for stocks not particularly overpriced in the beginning. These are times for profits.

Just because the market has underpriced a stock doesn't mean you should buy and hold it in your portfolio. As I emphasized in our previous discussions on asset allocation, any asset you buy should fulfill a purpose in your portfolio.

Reaching for quick profits can be risky, so don't use your retirement money for this purpose. You should also be aware of the tax consequences of quick profits. However, when framed the right way, a quick profit is a way to raise more cash for those securities you want to hold.

DON'T LOOK FOR THE BOTTOM

It doesn't make any sense to wait for the bottom of the market, because you won't see it until it has passed. Focus instead on a reasonable price for the stock: Where do you expect the stock to go?

Bottom feeders seldom find the bottom. They're just like the folks who want to sell at the absolute peak. Buy when the stock hits a price supported by the fundamentals of the business. Sell when you have made your profit target, or not at all if that is your strategy.

IDENTIFYING BARGAIN MUTUAL FUNDS

Finding bargains among mutual funds is different from "K-Marting" stocks. When you buy a stock, you should know what you're buying. That's not always the case with mutual funds. Funds may have a name that suggests one investment model, when they may actually invest in a whole different class of assets.

Fund managers may have wide latitude in where they place the fund's money. They may also use sophisticated investment tools such as options and futures contracts. This all makes it difficult to understand when a fund is performing well or poorly. Morningstar.com has a great deal of information on individual funds, and most of it is free. The Web site classifies funds by what they actually do with investors' money rather than what the fund's name suggests. This is very helpful in comparing one fund to other similar funds. They also include an appropriate index comparison.

In general terms, stock mutual funds experience net outflows during bear markets. This means they are redeeming more shares than investors are buying new shares. In other words, investors are pulling out of stock funds. This forces the managers to sell stock shares to cover the redemptions. In better times, new money coming in to the fund more than offsets the redemptions.

Right now, a good question might be: Who is still investing in stock mutual funds in the middle of a bear market? It's hard to know exactly, but a good deal of the money is probably coming from 401(k) and other retirement plans that automatically invest participants' contributions. A bear market may also leave some sectors of the economy relatively untouched. Funds that invest in these sectors, such as consumer staples, utilities, and so on, may do all right in a bear market.

If money is flowing out of stock funds, what happens to it? Frequently, you can track the money to bond or cash funds and some hybrid (bonds and stock) funds.

Unfortunately, the same situation with individual stocks afflicts mutual fund investors. They watch the fund drop well below what they paid before they bail out. When the market comes back, they watch the fund climb above where they sold and find themselves in the unfortunate position of selling low and buying high, which compounds their loss. Unless you get your money out before the carnage, you may be better off doing nothing, assuming your time horizon permits a wait for the market's return.

WHERE TO FIND BARGAINS

Mutual funds can produce bargains in a bear market, and there are several ways to take advantage of them. Use the same caution with mutual funds that we employed with stocks: Don't assume that because the fund has had a huge drop in share price that it is a bargain. The health of the underlying stocks is more important than other factors we considered for individual stocks.

For example, investor sentiment has less of an influence on mutual fund pricing than it does on individual stocks. Individual stocks trade a fixed number of shares. More buyers than sellers means the price per share rises; if a stock is hot, buyers drive up the price. If a mutual fund is hot, new money coming in doesn't change the share price. The reason is that mutual funds expand to accommodate as many investors as possible. There are some limits to how much new money a fund can handle, and some funds limit the amount of new money.

C a u t i o n

> Finding bargains in the mutual fund area can be difficult. Other factors (fees, expenses, taxes, and so on) besides the underlying value of the fund's holdings can affect the price per share.

NO PLACE LIKE HOME

If you already own a stock mutual fund, you may not have to look any further than your own portfolio. Assuming you don't need the money immediately, you may want to do nothing.

Research will tell you how the fund did in a normal market (not a bear or a bull) if the fund is old enough. If you are satisfied that you want to own the fund under that scenario, you might consider adding more to the fund on a monthly basis. This puts you in a dollar cost averaging mode of investing and can be particularly effective in unstable markets. You don't worry about where the bottom is because you're going to keep investing right through it and into the upturn.

A note of caution: If the fund is tech-laden, don't expect a big rebound when the market turns, and certainly don't expect it to return to the glory days of the late 1990s. Stock funds that invested in a broad cross-section of industries and index funds may be your best bets.

VALUE FUNDS

Value funds are just what the name implies: funds that look for undervalued stocks. The strategy is to buy cheap and sell expensive as the stocks move up to a more realistic value.

Value funds do what I suggested investors do with individual stocks. They will undoubtedly be more efficient, but you always give up some gain due to mutual fund fees and so on.

Value funds may not perform all that well in the depths of a bear market, but when the market begins its upturn, expect some handsome gains.

Tip

If you just can't decide what to do, you are probably better off doing nothing. If you can't stand to watch your funds fall, sell your losers and put the money in a money-market fund, bond, or other cash instrument.

SECTOR FUNDS

Sector funds invest heavily in particular industries. They should never be a solo investment, but used in connection with a well-balanced portfolio.

However, during a bear market, sector funds that focus on industries that aren't at the top of the bear's menu may be an appealing buy for a small portion of your portfolio.

THE BEST DEFENSE IS A GOOD OFFENSE

As I mentioned earlier, a bear market may be a good time to put money into the market, as opposed to taking it out. By the spring of 2001, investors considered surviving Internet/tech stocks as values. Intel, Cisco, and Microsoft had all taken big hits in the bear sell-off, yet these companies represent the cream of tech stocks. Funds that focus on large cap tech stocks might be good buys.

It is doubtful these stocks will quickly recover all the ground they lost, but you don't care. If the fund buys at depressed prices, the stocks don't have to move back to their old highs for a good profit.

Dollar cost averaging into these funds may be a good long-term strategy for picking up a large number of fund shares at low prices before the market comes back.

CONCLUSION

Bear markets can be times of great concern for investors. However, there are always opportunities for profits in any market. Investors need to adjust their thinking and expectations to deal with bear markets. Most folks would be happy to come out of a bear market close to even. If you can pick up some bargains and convert them into profits, you may offset losses in other areas.

PART 5

BEAR DEN

The period beginning when you realize that retirement is not very far away and continuing into retirement is a dangerous time for investors. Just when the thought of retreating from the front lines of employment starts sounding better every day, a bear jumps out of the woods and takes a bite out of your future income.

Bear markets can strike at any time, and the closer you are to needing money from your investments, the more your portfolio is at risk.

As we discussed earlier, pulling out of the market too soon can also be costly. In this part of the book, we will be looking at specific strategies for pre-retirement and post-retirement. We will also discuss some of the "safe" places you can sock away some money.

CHAPTER 16

PRE-RETIREMENT STRATEGIES

Our parents called retirement the "golden years," but now we know them as the "anxiety years." The reason is that so many retirement plans tie ultimate benefits to investing decisions made by individual workers.

As you approach retirement, be aware that you probably need to make some fundamental changes in your portfolio. With any luck, you will be able to make these changes in normal market situations.

DANGEROUS TIMES

Earlier in this book, we talked about the length and recovery of bear markets reaching back 70-plus years. Those numbers should chill you to the bone if you are beginning your pre-retirement planning. A major reversal at the wrong time (assuming there ever is a right time) can mean the difference between a retirement of fun and relaxation and one spent worrying about outliving your money.

Caution

If you have a 20-plus year retirement, it's almost a certainty that one or more bear markets will attack your portfolio.

Bear markets do happen, and there's no way to predict whether they will be close together or spread out with periods of bull markets in between. Preparation is your best defense, especially if you start during a normal market.

PRE-RETIREMENT CHECKLIST

When you start your preparations for retirement is a personal choice, but I would start within 7 to 10 years of retirement, depending on the current market and what the future looks like. This gives you time to slowly rebalance your portfolio to more accurately reflect your retirement posture and fill in any holes that may exist.

Here are some points to consider during pre-retirement:

- If you have an investment portfolio and a retirement portfolio (and I hope you do), consider them together but with different roles.

- Make sure you understand your retirement plan and its withdrawal rules. Generally, the IRS requires you to begin withdrawals at a certain age. Since this age is subject to change, your tax professional can tell you the rules that apply in your situation. You also need to understand the distribution options, especially for pension plans.

- You may have more than one retirement plan. If you had a 401(k) or other qualified plan from a previous employer, you probably rolled it into an IRA when you left. This plan becomes part of the mix, too.

- Check with the Social Security Administration for an estimate of your benefits and any rules that may apply to working after retirement.

- Consider hiring a financial professional if you don't already have professional help.

These are some of the major investment and planning steps you need to consider. Of course, there are other concerns, such as paying off all or a substantial portion of any debt, preparing or updating your will, polishing your golf clubs, and so on. Let's expand on some of those points.

INVESTMENT AND RETIREMENT PORTFOLIOS

If you planned well, you have both an investment portfolio and a retirement portfolio. When it comes to facing a bear market, you may want to treat these portfolios differently. Bear markets aren't the only consideration, however. Taxes, both capital gains and income; inflation; and general economic instability are forces to contend with also.

Your investment portfolio presents you with some serious tax concerns. If you sell large pieces at a profit for living expenses during a bear market, you will generate tax bills. Withdrawals from a qualified retirement account generate taxes as ordinary income. You avoid all the capital gains associated with nonqualified accounts. As I write this, the capital-gains tax is 20 percent on securities if held for at least one year. If you anticipate a higher income tax bracket than 20 percent after retirement, you may be better off paying the capital-gains tax. (Of course, if you invested in a Roth IRA, your withdrawals are tax-free.)

When you do your pre-retirement planning, think about which accounts you withdraw from first. Consult a tax professional before making any decisions.

T i p

Roth IRAs are a special type of retirement account that lets you put after-tax dollars in an account that builds tax-free. When you begin withdrawals, they are also tax-free.

You should also consider the composition of your investment account. If it contains a significant percentage of growth stocks, a bear market could inflict heavy damage. The asset-allocation models we looked at in Chapter 13, "Age-Appropriate Strategies," suggested a move toward more predictable returns as you approach retirement. However, inflation and the possibility of another 20-plus years of living expenses after retirement make a complete retreat from the market unwise.

UNDERSTAND YOUR RETIREMENT PLAN

A cliché I often hear is "Your house is your biggest asset." That is absolutely wrong. Your biggest and most important asset is what you've put away for retirement. This asset has to last you for the rest of your life, which, presumably, you hope is a long time. How you manage it before your actual retirement will determine how well you will enjoy your "golden years." (Manage it poorly and you may find yourself saying, "You want fries with that burger?")

Your first step is getting a firm handle on what your particular plan offers in terms of a payout. Can you roll it into an IRA? What about dumping a lump sum into an annuity?

T i p

> Estimating your income and expenses during retirement is complicated. Bear markets can throw your estimates off on the income side. Inflation can play havoc with expense estimates.

The worst thing that can happen is you have to make an uninformed decision at retirement and it costs you a chunk of your nest egg. You should have an estimated payout a few years before retirement and a well-designed plan to deal with the proceeds. Your decision should consider all your assets and how "bear exposed" you are.

There are rules regarding withdrawals that could come into play in the middle of a bear market if you're not careful. Tax laws change frequently, so please consult a professional before making any decisions on your own.

MULTIPLE RETIREMENT PLANS

If you've changed jobs a few times in your career, you may have rolled assets from retirement plans into an IRA(s). These need to be a part of your total retirement plan, with special attention paid to the type of assets you are holding in the IRA.

Many folks take an aggressive stance with their retirement accounts because they can avoid the capital-gains tax issues while the assets are in the account. Remember that bears love growth stocks and funds. Take a hard look at how much damage you are willing to risk in order to stay invested in the market as an inflation hedge.

CHECK WITH SOCIAL SECURITY ADMINISTRATION

Before retirement gets too close, check with Social Security on the status of your account. They can provide you with a statement including an estimate of benefits when you retire.

It's also important to check the accuracy of your report in time to get something done before you start drawing monthly payments.

HIRE A PROFESSIONAL TO HELP YOU PLAN

Your pre-retirement planning sets up your standard of living for the rest of your life. When you consider all your assets, even people with modest incomes may have amassed many hundreds of thousands of dollars in net worth.

Although this may seem like a large sum of money, it has to last the rest of your life. Now is not the time to "do it yourself." Retirement planning under the best of circumstances is a complicated process. When you add in the almost certainty of one or more bear markets, it may seem overwhelming. I feel strongly that you should hire a professional to help draw up a plan for financing your retirement, someone to look at the whole picture—not just your investments but other considerations such as insurance and so on.

Caution

A retirement-planning professional can help you put together a plan that considers all the variables and outlines a course of action to achieve your retirement goals.

Ideally, this plan will be in place before you retire so there are no decisions about pension plan payouts and rollovers. This professional should specialize in retirement planning and work on a fee-only basis. Many companies that provide investment products will help you with retirement planning, but I'm not convinced their recommendations always have your best interests in mind.

A CPA or other financial professional can put together a comprehensive plan for your retirement that considers the whole picture. You will pay several thousand dollars or more depending on how complicated your situation is, but it will be the best money you ever spent. Express your concern about bear markets, and the professional will factor it into the plan.

Don't cheat yourself out of a hard-earned retirement by guessing how to organize your assets or letting a bear market take a big percentage away from you.

DANGEROUS TIMING

You can use your pre-retirement years to get your financial life organized, so by the time you're ready for a well-earned permanent vacation, you won't have to spend extra time worrying about how to pay for it.

No one plans for a stock market disaster just before retirement, but it happens. My experience is that planning is very important if you hope to accomplish a goal, but you need to be flexible enough to adapt to sudden and unexpected changes.

Bear markets can play havoc with your pre-retirement planning, and they almost always come at the worst time. In Chapter 13, we discussed the process of gradually moving your portfolio from a growth posture to a more secure posture. This helps you move out of volatile assets over time and can eliminate some of the concern that you may need to cash in a mutual fund at the bottom of a bear market.

Think of it as dollar cost averaging in reverse. Dollar cost averaging directs you to invest a fixed amount every month or so into the market. You invest regardless of the market's behavior. You buy more when it is down and less when it is up. I'm not suggesting you take out a fixed amount each month and move the proceeds to a more appropriate pre-retirement asset. I'm suggesting that realigning your portfolio and its priorities should be a gradual process.

On a practical note, cashing out all at once also generates some significant tax considerations. Spreading out the redemptions over several tax years can ease the load.

LOCK IN RETURNS

One benefit of realigning your portfolio in your pre-retirement years is to lock in returns on part of your assets. These fixed returns will give you a solid base. Bonds, CDs, money market accounts, and money market funds can help you do this. Money market accounts and funds are highly liquid, but their interest rates do fluctuate. Bonds and CDs are not as liquid, but you can lock in a return and feel confident about the security of your principal.

Bankrate.com is an excellent source for information on interest rates for various cash instruments. Your CD is as safe in an insured bank across the country as it is in the bank across town.

BONDS COME IN DIFFERENT FLAVORS

The two main attributes of bonds, fixed return and security of principal, are important antidotes to bear markets. One reason you use bonds to protect against a bear market is that they are not subject to market changes if you don't plan to trade them.

Trading bonds in the open market subjects them to interest-rate changes and market-demand influences. If you're concerned about locking in a return, stick with individual bonds you plan to hold to maturity. You can buy bonds in many different denominations and with a variety of maturities. In the previous section, I talked about realigning your portfolio gradually. Bonds are ideal candidates for this situation.

For example, say you have $20,000 in a growth mutual fund and you are 55 years old. You want to take some of the fluctuations out of your portfolio common to this type of fund, but you want to stay in the market as long as possible, so the fund can work for you. If you take $2,000 out of the fund every year and buy a bond with a five- to seven-year maturity, you have shifted part of your assets out of the bear's reach and into an asset that normally has a reasonable return.

Of course, if you see the bear coming, you can accelerate the process.

THE DOWNSIDE OF INDIVIDUAL BONDS

Buying individual bonds isn't difficult, but it's not quite as painless as buying stocks or mutual funds. You need a broker with experience and connections in the bond market. Many consumers balk at the often complex pricing and commission schedules of bonds. However, do a little homework and you should be set.

You don't have to buy a newly issued bond to meet your maturity requirements. Your broker will explain how the secondary market prices. If you want to sell your bond before maturity, you may or may not get a good price for it depending on interest rates and market demand. Trading bonds eliminates the stability you need to counteract a bear market.

Caution

> Trading bonds removes the stabilizing influence they can have on your portfolio and puts them in the same category as stocks, subject to market variances.

BOND MUTUAL FUNDS

Many investors prefer bond mutual funds to individual bonds. They are just like stock mutual funds in that they buy and sell bonds looking for a certain return. The attributes of bonds dictate the structure of the fund. For example, you can find short-, medium-, and long-maturity bond funds as well as tax-exempt bond funds.

A large number of bond funds offer a variety of goals and benefits. In general, bond funds offer more liquidity than individual bonds. However, bond funds don't assure you of a rate of return or that your principal will be intact when you need it (if the bond market sours, bond funds share price falls). If you want to be sure that a precise sum of money is available on a certain date, individual bonds held to maturity are the answer.

This is why you use bonds as a hedge against bear markets. Individual stocks and mutual funds (stock, bond, or both) can't make that assurance. Bonds give you a firm basis to defend yourself from bear attacks.

Full disclosure: Yes, bonds do default. However, if you use a reputable broker, that risk is almost zero.

THE IMPORTANCE OF CASH

The title of this section may seem a little silly. Of course, cash is important. The point goes beyond the obvious to a more practical defense against bear markets.

Your pre-retirement planning must include an estimate of your living expenses. What do you need each month to pay for utilities, the phone, groceries, and the other basics? How much beyond that do you want to spend on recreational activities?

These two numbers make up your cash needs for retirement. As you shift assets in the pre-retirement years, make sure you can easily cover the basics without dipping into your principal if possible. This may help you weather a bear market without selling assets at a loss after retirement. It is possible to curtail your recreational activities to avoid selling in a down market, but it may not be possible to curtail your basic needs.

Tip

> Don't go overboard and put everything in cash. Inflation reduces the value of cash by raising prices.

Cash gives you the option of avoiding selling assets in a bear market unless you absolutely have to cover an unexpected expense.

CONCLUSION

The planning and preparation you do in your pre-retirement years will determine the quality of your retirement. If you take only one thing away from this chapter, I hope it is that hiring a retirement-planning professional is the smartest, and ultimately cheapest, move you can make.

CHAPTER 17

RETIREMENT PROTECTION

I live where bears (real bears, not market ones) can be a problem. Most of the incidents occur farther north, but bear sightings and problems can happen anywhere. I've never had a problem with the bears, but every year, bears ravage campsites, destroy trashcans, and, occasionally, chew up hikers and hunters. This has given me a healthy respect for what bears can do.

This is a roundabout way of warning you that investors must also respect bears—market bears and real ones. Market bears demand the most respect just before and during retirement. The previous chapter detailed some of the precautions and planning necessary to prepare your bear defense.

I don't mean to be an alarmist or to frighten you about bear markets during your retirement. I do want to help you prepare for the bear market(s) that will surely come sometime during your retirement. There is no guaranteed bear repellent, and some bears and accompanying recessions can be so bad that no one will escape unharmed. With proper planning, however, you can hope to prevent serious damage. This section and the rest of the book will help you formulate your plan.

NO MARGIN FOR ERROR

There I go again, being an alarmist. However, I don't think I'm overstating the seriousness of the situation by stressing that a major error during retirement can change the rest of your life. Do you remember our lady friend from the first chapter? She didn't pay attention to her portfolio, and a bear market took half of it just before her retirement. Would it be fair to say that event changed her life?

Retirement should be a time when you have options about how you spend your time and live your life. In the last chapter, I encouraged you to use a professional planner to help you prepare for retirement. This may be the most important decision you make in regards to securing a solid retirement. This book and others like it can only provide general guidance and information.

Every person's particular retirement situation is different. A professional planner can translate the principles discussed here into a real plan that specifically addresses your needs and concerns. I recommend a fee-only professional to avoid any undue influence product commissions might have on a proposed plan.

TWO OPPOSITE PROBLEMS

Ironically, retirees face two opposite choices: being too conservative and being too aggressive. Either one can cause big problems for your retirement. If you're too conservative with your investments during retirement, you risk outliving your money. If you're too aggressive with your investments, a bear market may rob you of a substantial portion of your portfolio. Add to this the problem of having enough but not too much cash, and it's easy to understand why professional planners earn their fees.

Tip ————————————————————————————————

> The proper balance between a portfolio that is too conservative and one that is too aggressive is the heart of a retirement plan that takes advantage of continued appreciation with sufficient safeguards.

TOO CONSERVATIVE

In the previous chapter, I talked about the importance of moving some of your assets into bonds and/or cash instruments to cover living expenses during a bear market so you wouldn't have to sell off assets at depressed prices. You might be tempted to convert everything to bonds and cash, so you don't have to worry about bear markets.

Tempting as this sounds, it has problems of its own. Even if inflation stays at its recent low of about 3 percent a year, that's enough to erode your cash stash much quicker than you think. For example, say you convert your assets to cash and invest $500,000 in a fixed-return instrument like a CD or bond that pays 6 percent per year. You estimate the $30,000 of income each year will be enough to cover expenses.

This seems like a simple plan—except inflation will rob you of 3 percent each year. Instead of $30,000 per year for expenses, you have less each year in purchasing power. After 10 years, your $30,000 per year will now only buy just over $22,000 per year in goods and services. Subtract income taxes and the figure would even be lower.

I chose to use a 6 percent return in this simple example on purpose. It's twice the 3 percent inflation rate of the recent past, and it illustrates that earning even twice the inflation rate isn't enough to hold off the drain on your retirement cash.

This is why the Fed and everyone else fears inflation. People on fixed incomes suffer the most during inflation, and adopting a too-conservative posture can be devastating. Inflation will eat away at your earnings, and the only way you can compensate is to reduce spending.

Caution

> Inflation, even at a modest rate, can destroy a fixed-income budget over time. Protection against its effect means leaving at least part of your portfolio invested as a hedge.

The point is that to stay even, your investments must earn the rate of inflation and then some—but protecting yourself from inflation can leave you open to other problems, not the least of which are bear attacks. In the past, large cap stocks have proven that they can grow faster than the rate of inflation. They are also targets of bear markets. During a few days of wild bear trading in March 2001, the Dow (all large cap stocks) lost over 1,000 points.

AN UNLIKELY FRIEND

Although unlikely, deflation can be your friend in retirement. You'll remember from earlier discussions that deflation occurs when too many goods are chasing too few dollars. Cash becomes more valuable than goods and prices fall. People on fixed incomes can do very well in deflation because their fixed income increases in value over time.

Deflation is probably the least likely reason we will have a bear market, but events in Japan for the 10 years leading up to early 2001 indicate it is possible. As I write this, their equivalent of the U.S. Fed is providing Japan's banks with zero-interest loans to keep the entire system from collapsing.

Could that happen here? Probably not, but as the world's economies grow more entwined through globalization, the possibility exists for massive economic disruptions.

NO PAIN, NO GAIN

The asset-allocation models we looked at earlier in Chapter 13, "Age-Appropriate Strategies," provided for some participation in the stock market even after retirement except in the most conservative models.

Unless you have a very large retirement nest egg and very modest plans after retirement, most of you will still need the growth stocks provide to see you through. That extra post-retirement growth may make a big difference in how long your money lasts and how you can spend it. Without that growth, you may need to work some after retirement whether you planned to or not.

Those folks with a high aversion to risk might find this necessity painful. That's perfectly understandable, but you need to find a way that is as comfortable as possible to accomplish the goal of continued growth after retirement.

T i p ───────────────────────────────────────

> Many investors find mutual funds a convenient and safe way to invest
> in stocks. Professional managers take on the burden of evaluating indi-
> vidual companies as investments.

Mutual funds are the safest way to stay invested in equities. They offer
professional management and most provide a level of diversification individual investors can't achieve. Mutual fund managers should also be better prepared in the event of a bear market. Hybrid funds that invest in
stocks and bonds may be a good choice for low-risk investors.

TOO AGGRESSIVE

Investors who are too aggressive after retirement expose themselves to
more risk than is prudent by most standards. These folks often fall into
two groups:

- Those like our lady friend in Chapter 1, "Bear Markets," who just
  didn't pay any attention to her portfolio before retirement and lost
  a big piece of it in a bear market.
- Those investors who believe they can jump out of the way (just in
  time) of a charging bear.

Their portfolios suffer the same result: They rob themselves of a better life
in retirement.

START PAYING ATTENTION

Investors who don't pay attention and lose part of their retirement portfolio to a bear market have no one but themselves to blame. Many resources are available to help you understand the basics of investing,
including books (such as *Alpha Teach Yourself Investing in 24 Hours*),
Internet sites, and educational programs offered locally in many commu-
nities.

If you have neither the time nor the patience to handle these decisions on your own, consider using the services of a professional. Fee-based
financial planners will help you devise a strategy that you can follow on
your own with periodic updates.

Tip ——————————————————————————————

> Financial planners usually carry a professional designation such as CFP (Certified Financial Planner) or ChFC (Chartered Financial Consultant). These designations mean the planner has fulfilled specialized education requirements and met ethical and professional standards. The designations don't necessarily mean they are fee-only.

Some brokerage houses still offer investment services. Check to see if any of them have offices nearby; they'll be glad to put together an investment program that meets your needs and is appropriate for your age group. You'll pay fees and/or commissions for these services, but you may sleep better with someone else making the decisions and keeping an eye on the progress of the plan.

Investors who don't pay attention to the market or economy are too aggressive by default because they set up an investment pattern years ago and never changed it. Asset allocation and diversification are foreign terms to these investors. They sail into retirement with their assets in one or two instruments and with a big "Bite Me" sign on their back. Guess whom the bear is going after first?

The bear market that ate the Nasdaq in 2000 and 2001 feasted on investors who put all they had into tech stocks during the late 1990s. For a while, they looked like market geniuses, until the bear ate them for lunch. Don't let your portfolio suffer from lack of attention.

THE MARKET TIMER

The investor who believes he can quickly jump from in front of a charging bear is practicing market timing. In previous chapters, I made a strong case for avoiding the practice of market timing—just because you may have more time in retirement to spend watching every tic of the market doesn't mean you will be any more successful than before you retired.

Professionals, who spend their whole life watching the market, can't do market timing with consistent success. You can't either. In fact, spending your days watching the market's every gesture may be worse than not watching it at all. There is too much information coming in at one time to be meaningful. The microanalysis of the stock market on a minute-by-minute basis, like you find on cable television and Internet sites, fed the hysteria that created the Internet/tech bubble in the late 1990s. This same microanalysis helped fan the panic selling, which began with the tech-rich Nasdaq in April of 2000 and spread to the rest of the market in early 2001.

Tip —————————————————————————————

Changing technology and information sources may have long-term influences on the stock market we haven't even begun to understand. Micromanaging your portfolio is no guarantee of success. People who actively trade run up commission charges and tax bills, often for little gain.

My grandfather had a saying about spending too much time worrying about a decision: "You study long, you study wrong." (I usually heard this while trying to figure my next move in a game of dominoes with him.) In the best of worlds, you have a plan in place before the bear attacks, and you already know the next move. When it comes time to make decisions, having goals and objectives identified will keep you focused on those areas of highest priority.

BEND IN THE WIND

I'm sure you've heard the old cliché that trees that bend in a windstorm are more likely to survive than trees that stand rigid. Being flexible in the face of adversity is important. Have a plan for your retirement nest egg, because even the best plans can't allow for every circumstance.

Technology has given us the opportunity to retrieve, analyze, and act on information almost instantly. Half of all households in America have a stake in the stock market through direct investing or retirement plans. This unprecedented set of circumstances may change the way markets react to major economic events, and we don't know what those changes will mean. How will bear markets be different in the future? What challenges will we face because of this new set of circumstances?

Retirees should be prepared to adjust their plans if a new type of bear rears its ugly head. Safe havens for investors, which we will discuss more in the next chapter, may no longer be safe. For example, real estate is a traditional haven from market woes, yet if deflation becomes a serious problem, it will be a terrible safety net in a bear market.

What you thought was a fairly conservative investment when you bought it may have turned into a much more aggressive stock or mutual fund. Individual stocks are the most likely to change as companies evolve in the market and take on new directions or drop old product lines. Mutual funds can also change their focus and move from one level of risk to another.

A helpful tool is the Portfolio Manager on Morningstar.com. You can create a portfolio of the holdings you question, and the Portfolio Manager will give you detailed information, including how conservative or aggressive your holdings are. This is very helpful if you are planning to rebalance your portfolio and build a bear defense.

OUTLIVE THE BEAR

"The best revenge is a long life." This proverb could describe a perfect strategy for dealing with a bear market. One of the ways you can get past a bear market is to simply outlive it. Of course, you don't know how long it will last, so this strategy is not without flaws.

In the previous chapter, I talked about cash and how important it is in allowing you to avoid drawing down on your principal. This is where that strategy can work to defeat a bear market. You should have a "Plan B" that addresses ways to reduce expenses or even increase income during a bear market. The longer you can avoid cashing in investments at depressed prices, the longer your investments can continue to work for you.

T i p ————————————————————————————————————

> Plan for the possibility that a bear market can be defeated or at least severely wounded by cutting back on expenses to put off cashing in investments at depressed prices.

With some careful planning and a little luck, you might be able to get through all but the lengthiest bear markets without cashing in depressed investments. Even if you eventually have to cash in some investments, a prudent cash plan can postpone that necessity. The longer you can keep your investments in the market, the better chance you have that the bear will die and the market will turn up. You can then sell fewer shares and raise more cash.

CONCLUSION

You are most vulnerable to bear markets during your retirement years when you are relying on investment income to pay the bills. Retirees often live 20-plus years past retirement, which means they will almost certainly face one or more bear markets. A well-planned retirement that takes special care to provide adequate cash is your best defense against a bear market.

CHAPTER 18

SAFE HAVENS

A friend once explained to me a reaction to Chaos Theory that he learned in the army:

When in danger,
When in doubt;
Run in circles,
Scream and shout!

The chaos of the stock market can certainly encourage one to follow my friend's reaction. However, most of us look for more constructive ways to deal with the uncertainty of market turmoil.

As I've said repeatedly: The most important way you can protect your assets from bear markets and other nasty surprises is to have a well-diversified portfolio. Correctly allocating assets relative to your goals, risk tolerance, and time horizon prepares you for most of the bad things that happen in the market.

There are times when you need a "safe haven" to ride out a market storm or take an extra measure of protection for your portfolio. The term "safe haven" implies someplace you can put assets with no fear of harm. Unfortunately, "safe" in this case is somewhat relative. Most truly safe places to put your money always involve giving up a substantial amount of return in exchange.

This chapter looks at some of the "safe havens" available to investors. You can use them for a variety of reasons. The most common reason is to avoid the clutches of a bear market.

BONDS

Bonds are a traditional part of virtually every asset-allocation model. A bond is simply an I.O.U. or debt from an organization. Various governmental units and corporations issue bonds. They are as safe as the organization issuing the bond. They provide a measure of stability for your portfolio's equities.

One of the safest moves you can make is increasing the bond component of your portfolio. We have discussed this in the asset-allocation discussions. Bonds provide a fixed rate of return and an assurance of principal if you hold them to maturity. Along with cash, bonds add a stabilizing influence to your stock portfolio.

Several independent services rate bonds against the possibility of default. The greater the possibility of default, the higher interest rate the issuer must pay.

U.S. TREASURY ISSUES

U.S. Treasury bonds are a great place to park cash until the need to use it arises. They offer absolute safety and a fixed rate of return and are exempt from state and local taxes.

However, the low rate of return that accompanies this safety means you may be essentially parking the money for no return by the time you factor in taxes and inflation. Bear markets can't hurt these bonds. The risk they present is lost opportunity costs associated with not having your assets invested in the market when it returns.

Lost opportunity costs are the profits you miss because your money is tied up in a safe but low-return investment. Quality investments will score significant increases when the market leaves bear country, but you will miss those gains if your money is tied up elsewhere. That is the "cost" you pay for safety.

T i p

> Treasury bonds are absolutely safe if held to maturity. You will get your principal back plus interest. This feature is often more important than high rates of return.

There is some upside to Treasury bonds. If interest rates fall while you are holding a bond, you may be able to sell it at a premium. This comes in handy when the danger has passed and you're ready to move the money back into the equity market. Of course, the opposite is also true. If interest rates rise while you're holding the bond, you may have to discount it on the open market. As you can see, the minute you trade Treasury bonds, the absolute guarantee disappears. Market conditions may dictate that you discount the bond to sell it.

If you only need a holding place for a short time, consider one of the very short (one year and under) maturity Treasury issues. These pay the lowest interest rate, but you only have to hold them a short time until maturity to get your full principal back.

U.S. AGENCY BONDS

A number of U.S. government agencies issue bonds to finance a variety of services, including mortgages and student loans. These bonds usually pay more than U.S. Treasury issues, but they do not carry the "full faith and credit" of the U.S. Government. They are only slightly more risky than Treasury issues. Specific assets like houses back the bonds.

Some of the more familiar U.S. agency bonds include Ginnie Mae (GNMAs), Fannie Mae (FNMAs), and Freddie Mac (FHLs). These bonds range in maturity from 1 month to 20 years. You are fairly secure in using agency bonds as a safe place for hiding from bears. They are exempt from state and local taxes.

Tip ──

There are special municipal bonds that are tax-free including federal, state, and local taxes. There are mutual funds that specialize in these issues.

MUNI'S

State, county, city, and other local agencies issue municipal bonds or muni's. Independent services rate the issuers for creditworthiness. Tax revenues and other income sources back these bonds. Municipalities issue the bonds in large denominations ($5,000 and up).

They are less secure than U.S. Treasury or agency issues, but highly rated muni's seldom default. They are exempt from federal income tax.

CORPORATE BONDS

Companies issue bonds to finance business growth, especially new plants and equipment. Companies sometimes use bonds to finance acquisitions. Companies may prefer bonds to commercial loans because the company can structure longer pay-offs and better interest rates.

Independent services rank corporate bond issues also, and the interest rate is determined from the credit rating. Corporate bonds are more risky than U.S. Treasury bonds because bad economic times can affect the company's ability to repay.

If you're using bonds to cushion your portfolio during bear markets, corporate bonds may not be the answer. Bear markets in connection with a recession could put a strain on the company to repay the bonds.

Caution ──

Corporate bonds that are poorly rated by independent services are not appropriate when safety is a primary concern.

Safety is a prime concern when investing in bonds, and corporate bonds are not necessarily the safest haven of all bonds.

BOND MUTUAL FUNDS

There are a number of mutual funds that invest in bonds. You can find just about any combination of yield and maturity you want in bond funds, which are easier and usually less expensive to buy than individual bonds. Professional managers make the decisions for you and follow the market more closely than you ever could.

You can get started in bond funds for a small initial deposit. Individual bonds often require significant sums to buy. You can also contribute small monthly amounts like stock funds, which makes getting into bonds very convenient.

Bond funds as part of your asset-allocation model make a lot of sense for all the reasons I just cited. However, if you are very conservative or absolutely need a certain sum of money at a future date, bond funds may not be for you. Bond funds trade bonds constantly. When they do, it opens the fund to the possibility of losses, just like equity funds.

If you buy a one-year, $10,000 U.S. Treasury bond, at the end of the year you will get your $10,000 back for sure. If you put $10,000 in a bond fund, in one year you may not get $10,000 back when you need it. Of course, you may get more than $10,000 back if the fund does well.

That's the difference between buying and holding a bond to maturity and trading bonds on the open market. Holding a bond to maturity is a reasonable guarantee that you will get your entire principal. Trading bonds, whether individually or within a mutual fund, exposes you to the possibility of loss or gain.

Bond funds work well in your asset-allocation model; however, if you absolutely need the principal intact, then individual bonds held to maturity are the answer.

Bonds are an important part of any well-diversified portfolio. You can accomplish this part of diversification using individual bonds or a bond mutual fund. When you must protect the principal at all costs, U.S. Treasury bonds held to maturity are the answer.

REAL ESTATE

Real estate is one of those "hard" assets investors flock to when inflation threatens. In an inflationary environment, real estate will usually keep pace.

Investing in real estate is complicated and requires huge amounts of capital and time. Once you own real estate, it's hard to get rid of. In the words of a banker, real estate is an "illiquid" asset, meaning you can't easily convert it to cash.

Fortunately, you don't have to go through all this to own the benefits of real estate. Real estate investment trusts (REITs) and real estate mutual funds are the answer to all the difficulties of owning real estate.

REITS

REITs are a special breed of investment. They are more closely related to closed-end mutual funds, but they trade like equities on the stock exchange.

REITs invest in income-producing properties, such as shopping centers, apartments, and other commercial real estate. They receive income in the form of rent. Despite their specialized nature, REITs trade on major stock exchanges. This gives their shares liquidity or the ability of the owner to convert them to cash easily. Not all REITs trade as freely as others do. Some may be "thinly traded," meaning there isn't much of a market for the shares. If you want to sell these shares, you might find it difficult to get a good price—or any price.

REITs are popular during unstable markets when investors are looking for something of value. They did very well in 2000 when every major index closed down for the year: Periods of uncertainty in the stock market drive investors to look for alternative investments, and investors diving for cover from the Internet/tech sector found not only a safe place but a profitable one. However, real estate is not immune from the problems of recession and will drop in value like everything else.

REITs often act differently than equities during a turbulent market and may move in opposite directions. Their income derives from rents paid by tenants in the properties they own. Regular companies, on the other hand, sell products and services for their income. REITs must pay out 90 percent of their income, which means a steady flow of income to shareholders.

Tip

> REITs that specialize in particular types of investments give you the opportunity to pick the type of property that seems poised for the greatest growth.

Deflation will be bad news for REITs, as will a rapidly rising market. Deflation causes prices to drop as money becomes scarce. A rapidly rising market presents too many other good opportunities, so investors dump REITs in favor of growth stocks.

REAL ESTATE MUTUAL FUNDS

Another way to get into real estate is through mutual funds that invest in REITs. The main advantage to investing through a fund rather than directly into the REIT is liquidity.

With mutual funds, liquidity is not the problem it can be with thinly traded REITs. In addition, you get all the other benefits of mutual funds: professional managers and diversification.

Before you add REITs or real estate mutual funds to your portfolio, take a close look at any value funds you own. Value funds sometimes pick up REITs in their investments. You may already have coverage of real estate in your existing funds. You will probably have to ask for the fund's holdings, since funds report real estate investments in the "finance" section on most services. Contact the fund for more information.

Caution

> Many financial advisors suggest you put a small portion of your portfolio in foreign stocks, since they may not follow U.S. markets into the teeth of a bear. Buying individual foreign stocks is getting easier, but I recommend beginning investors stick with mutual funds that invest in foreign economies.

INTERNATIONAL FUNDS

Although it may strike some as odd that investors would look overseas for protection against a bear market in the U.S., that is exactly what some advisors do recommend.

Globalization is blurring the economic lines between national economies. However, overseas markets are rapidly developing markets with much room for future growth. You may be better off with a fund that targets medium to small foreign firms. Large multinational companies tend to move together.

International funds may provide some relief during turbulent domestic markets. I would not classify them as "safe havens" per se, just alternatives during down U.S. markets. Even then, I would not let international funds exceed 5 to 10 percent of your portfolio. While individuals can buy shares of stock in foreign companies, I believe most investors are better off turning those decisions over to professional managers of mutual funds.

INVESTING IN SECTORS

As we saw earlier, some sectors do better than others in a bear market. These sectors may not have the glamour of the Internet/tech arena, but they turn in steady performances in almost any market or economic conditions.

The following sectors offer some protection from bears in certain circumstances. You should consider mutual funds that follow these sectors volatile and probably not long-term investments but rather brief retreats. Individual stocks in these sectors require careful analysis to make sure they will follow sector trends.

Caution

Investing in economic sectors can be risky since you are not taking advantage of diversification. However, for a small part of your portfolio, they can provide a hedge against losses in the broad market for a limited time.

FINANCE

Falling interest rates usually help the finance sector by stimulating activity in home building and other credit-intensive activities.

Banks and other institutions that lend money do better in an environment of lowering interest rates, which might occur when the Fed tries to head off a recession. However, the financial sector may not benefit from falling interest rates if consumers are concerned about an economic slowdown.

UTILITIES

Utilities are favorite hiding places for many investors. They are traditionally very conservative investments that find their way into many retirement portfolios. Investors like them for their higher than average dividends, which have more value in a falling market with falling interest rates.

Not all utilities are equal—or managed well, for that matter. Deregulation and heavy debts from replacing aging facilities have strained some utilities. Utilities in California suffered disastrous consequences of a misguided deregulation that they themselves pushed for in early 2001.

The lesson is to pick wisely. A mutual fund that specializes in utilities may be a good bet, although the dividend issue is a problem.

CONSUMER STAPLES

Consumer staples include items like food and basic necessities. This sector is one of the most unglamorous, yet it keeps moving forward even in the midst of a bear market. Economic downturns have little effect on this sector since people still need to eat and wear clothes. Earnings may not grow at a fast rate, but this sector is a favorite safe haven for many bear-market veterans.

T i p

> Consumer staples are the bread and butter (pardon the pun) of many conservative asset-allocation models. Companies in this sector don't show rapid growth or super increases in earnings.

This is not a sector to stay with for the long term. When the economy picks up, these stocks are not going to grow much faster than during a recession. (People probably don't eat a lot more in an expanding economy). Investors often dump these funds in favor of growth-oriented investments.

HEALTHCARE

Healthcare is another favorite of investors during bear markets and recession. HMOs and drug companies are among the companies represented in this sector. Even in a down economy, people still get sick and buy drugs or go to the hospital.

This sector has a little more upside than consumer staples, thanks to increases in elective procedures (laser eye surgery and hair transplants, for example).

PRECIOUS METALS

Precious metals are a traditional hiding place from inflation. Along with real estate, precious metals were the weapon of choice in the 1970s and 1980s when inflation was high.

These stocks and funds have long been out of favor, thanks to an effective lid on inflation. You can be sure, however, that if inflation mounts a serious threat, investors will run to gold.

C a u t i o n

> Some bear market funds use shorting as their primary investment model. When the market is sliding into a bottomless pit, these funds do very well. However, when the market turns they may find themselves scrambling to stay alive. Approach with caution.

BEAR MARKET FUNDS

The most direct response to a bear market is to invest in mutual funds designed to profit from it. These funds come in several forms; however, they basically bet against the market by shorting growth stocks and stock indexes that will probably decline in a bear market.

Most of these funds are only a few years old and have no real track record to analyze. Most did well in 2000 and the beginning of 2001. You don't want to hold these funds when the market turns. They suffered massive losses during the bull market of the late 1990s.

These funds, especially those that try to achieve an inverse return of major indexes, are for short-term buys at best. When the market turns up, you'll want out of these funds fast. Unfortunately, you won't know when the market is truly turning up or just blipping before falling some more.

MARKET NEUTRAL FUNDS

The idea sounds great: Create a fund balanced in such a way that it profits regardless of whether the market is rising or falling. The fund invests in undervalued stocks and short overvalued stocks, and, no matter which way the market moves, the fund should achieve a target growth rate.

Unfortunately, practice and theory often produce different results. Few of the market neutral funds have performed up to expectations.

They require accurate and timely predictions of which stocks may go up and which stocks may go down. This is not foolproof by any means: Any fund that consistently requires managers to know which stocks are going up and down will have a hard time succeeding.

BALANCED FUNDS

Balanced or hybrid funds help you address the ratio of stocks to bonds in a single fund. These funds vary the ratio of stocks to bonds, so you can find one that is more conservative than another one.

One way to judge balanced funds is to look at some of the older ones and see how they fared in unstable markets of the past.

CONCLUSION

You can look at a number of alternatives when faced with a bear market that might help you weather the downturn. If you're young and have a long time horizon, you may be better off just riding it out. On the other hand, you may not want to sit passively when there are investment vehicles that might ease the pain.

Whatever measures you decide on, don't get completely out of the market. When the market turns up, you won't know it right away and will miss the early gains, which can be substantial.

PART 6

BEARSKIN RUG

Bears are dangerous because they are cunning and can move quickly. Your best defense against a bear market is preparing your portfolio in advance. This means you diversify your assets across stocks, bonds, and cash. This multi-pronged defense works on the theory that different assets move in opposite directions in certain market conditions.

Asset allocation addresses the proportions of each asset relative to your risk tolerance, time horizon, and financial goal.

Dollar cost averaging is a way to counterattack the bear market. It's the most effective tool the average investor can use.

CHAPTER 19

YOUR BEST BEAR STRATEGIES

Is a "buy-and-hold" strategy always the best answer in a bear market? Can dollar cost averaging really let you invest your way through a bear market? What other strategies can you use to survive a bear market?

I wish there were a better answer than "it depends." Of course, if the answer were simple, you wouldn't need this book! No pat answers will fit every investor in every down market. The number of variables is dramatic, and some of them are subjective and don't easily lend themselves to obvious answers.

In this chapter, I am going to look at some of the strategies I have mentioned in previous chapters. The idea is to help you come up with a strategy that fits your particular situation. You're more likely to follow a strategy consistently if you worked it out yourself than if you simply follow directions you don't really understand or believe.

BUY-AND-HOLD

The buy-and-hold strategy is almost carved in stone by some investors. It certainly has its strengths, but it has some flaws that you need to know about.

A long-term strategy works best when followed as your base invest-ing philosophy. This means you don't deviate from buy-and-hold without a very good reason. The strength of this strategy is that it keeps you in the market through the good times and the bad. Overall, you are better off invested than not.

On the other hand, buy-and-hold can be a disaster if you're in the wrong investment. Your money is not working for you if it is sitting in some stock or mutual fund that is going nowhere.

Here's a look at some of the positive and negative aspects of the buy-and-hold strategy.

BUY-AND-HOLD: PRO

The buy-and-hold strategy is one that many, if not most, investment pro-fessionals believe best suits the average investor. Some Wall Street tycoons have built their fortunes on this strategy.

The underlying reasoning of buy-and-hold is that over time you are better off invested in the stock market than not. This means you will do better if you put your money in and leave it because, over time, the stock market has been the most consistent investment you could make.

Two key elements make buy-and-hold work for you: a long-term view and quality investments. Actually, there is a third key element: the resolve to stick with the strategy when the market heads south. These el-ements work with the market's strengths to make your money work hard for you. Let's look at each one.

LONG-TERM VIEW

Although it went out of style during the 1990's bull market, the stock market has always been about long-term investing. The market works the most consistently over the long term.

Plenty of statistics reflect this positive aspect. One of my favorites is the fact that you can pick any 20-year period in the market's history, in-cluding the Great Depression, and "the market" has never lost a dime. (This statistic is through 1998.) It didn't matter where you got into the market as long as you stayed for 20 years. This points out the great strength the market has as a long-term investment. (I'm sure you can see some holes in this argument; however, I'll discuss those when I look at the weaknesses of buy-and-hold.)

Investors almost worship Warren Buffett as an investing guru. He identifies hidden jewels and buys them before the market discovers the stock and bids up the price. An interviewer asked the legendary investor how long was the proper holding period for an investment. Mr. Buffett answered, "Forever." Mr. Buffett made his fortune buying diamonds in the rough: companies that showed signs of future greatness and that the market undervalued. They became industry leaders and made Mr. Buffett a very wealthy man. (Of course, Mr. Buffett didn't hold *every* stock he bought forever, and this points out the other weakness of the buy-and-hold strategy. I'll talk about that more later, too.)

When you buy and hold a good stock for an extended period, you allow the company to grow at a natural pace. If you pick industry leaders as Mr. Buffett did, the effect of compounding growth is what makes buy and hold so potent. Great companies re-invest all or a substantial part of their earnings back into the company in the early years to finance growth. The market favors large companies. Over time, the large companies dominate their markets. This domination allows the company to make even more profits. A long period allows companies to grow and acquire market share. It lets them open new markets. Coca-Cola, one of Mr. Buffett's early successes, has huge operations outside the United States. According to Morningstar.com, 62 percent of the company's revenues come from operations outside North America.

GREAT COMPANIES

Investing in great companies is a key part of the buy-and-hold strategy. Great companies may stumble, but they do not fall. They lead markets out of bear territory. They continue to grow and innovate. They take advantage of market opportunities for new revenue sources. They forge alliances with strategic partners and swallow up competitors. Great companies open new markets overseas and domestically. They discontinue or sell off unprofitable ventures.

If you buy and hold great companies, you will profit from their continuing success. Even when they fall on hard times, they eventually work their way out of trouble.

BRANDING

Another benefit time buys companies is branding. Branding is the process of establishing a company's presence in the market. Branding makes McDonald's, IBM, and Coca-Cola household words not just in the United States, but around the world.

The dot.coms of the 1990s spent billions of dollars trying to build "brands." Some of them, like Amazon.com and Yahoo!, were successful, but the vast majority were not. Many of the New Economy order dismissed old brand identities as passé and not of great value. After the Internet/tech market flamed out, companies with a pre-Internet brand have done much better than the pure dot.coms.

What is a brand worth during a bear market? There's no easy answer, but we do know that investors are likely to stick close to companies they know.

MARKET TIMING

I have discussed in some detail the dangers of trying to time the market, which is impossible to repeat with any consistency. Another way to "time the market" is by staying invested. This keeps you in the market and means you will catch the first up-ticks of recovery.

Many recoveries make their biggest moves in the first 5 to 10 days. If you miss these days, you will miss the first burst of moves upward and reduce your overall gain. Investors who try to catch the first part of a recovery often miss it completely or mistake a "dead-cat bounce" for the recovery.

BUY-AND-HOLD: CON

The buy-and-hold strategy is widely accepted and praised as the best tool for individuals to accumulate wealth in the stock market. Investing in great companies for the long term is a sound strategy. However, there are some potentially dangerous flaws in the buy-and-hold strategy:

- The first and foremost potential flaw is the notion that individuals will consistently pick "great" companies.

- The second flaw is the notion of committing to the long-term hold. A commitment to a long-term hold can blind you to changes in the investment, market, and/or economy.

- Finally, the strategy relies on the investor remaining calm during a bear market and not selling in a panic to save something from the investment.

THE "GREAT" COMPANY FLAW

Every investor wants to invest in great companies. However, Mr. Buffett and other value investors didn't invest in companies that appeared "great" to the market.

Value investors look for companies undervalued by the market for reasons that have nothing to do with the fundamental soundness of the business. Many investors today associate high P/E ratios with greatness in a company. (Actually, all the P/E ratio shows is how expensive a stock is relative to the company's earnings.) I am very sure Coca-Cola didn't have a P/E ratio of 100 when Mr. Buffett began buying shares. Whatever it was selling for at the time, Mr. Buffett saw a bargain and the potential of something much greater.

Caution

> It is difficult to make a profit buying a stock at or near its historic high, even if you hold it for a long time.

One of the "great" companies of the 1990s bull market had a P/E of over 100 for several years and over 180 for one year. If you invested in this company at that level, you faced a rude awakening when the stock fell from a high of 82 to a low of 18. Even then, it still had a P/E of 46. How long is it going to take this "great" company to recover what it lost for investors? Is this stock a good buy now with a P/E of only 46?

There are only two ways a P/E can go down: The price of the stock has to fall, and/or the earnings have to increase. If this stock continues to fall and it manages to get earnings up, what is a good P/E to trigger a buy signal?

These are not fair questions because you need to know so much more about the company before you consider buying. Value investors never buy on just low P/E alone. Sometimes, a low P/E means the market is fairly valuing the stock.

THE "GREAT" COMPANY MYTH

The other problem with buying and holding "great" companies is they may not always be great companies. As I noted earlier, "great" companies that lost that mantle litter our history.

C a u t i o n

> Don't assume that a "great" company today will be a "great" company tomorrow. Things change and companies that don't change with the times are lost.

U.S. Steel still dominates the domestic steel industry, but there's not much left to dominate. Foreign competitors with significantly lower costs have eaten into the steel industry. It could barely muster $6 billion in sales in the 2000–2001 trailing 12-month period, compared to almost $24 billion for Microsoft in the same period.

Montgomery Ward, once a powerful retailer, filed for bankruptcy in 2000. The list goes on and on of once mighty companies reduced to secondary roles at best.

Things change and companies that can't change and profit from the change won't remain "great" companies for long.

THE LONG-TERM FLAW

The strong buy-and-hold followers suggest that once you buy that great stock, you should put the certificates in a deposit box and forget about them for 20 years or more. The problem is, just because you buy a truly great company at a great price and it remains a great company, that doesn't mean it's the best you could do with the money.

Great companies (and even not so great companies) can be down for 15 years and still turn a positive return to the 20-year holder. The problem is the lost opportunity costs of having your money in a nonproducing asset for many years when you could put it somewhere it will make money now.

Plain English

> **Opportunity costs** are those profits you lost because your money was in a nonproductive asset instead of one making you money.

This doesn't mean you have to become a day trader or a speculator. You can set price targets for your investments that they may reach in a short period or over a longer time span.

I discussed this strategy earlier. Some professionals suggest you have a price you want to sell at when you buy the stock. This strategy also has its flaws; for example, hitting your target may mean selling just as the stock was preparing to rise sharply.

COURAGE TO HANG ON

The buy-and-hold strategy requires a lot of courage: to sit tight through a tough bear market and watch your stock drop like a rock.

This may be the weakest link in the strategy. Investors without the necessary resolve often hold on as long as they can, then give up just when the investment has hit the bottom.

The unfortunate consequence is the investor has sold low and will probably have to pay more to get back in the market later.

THE BUY-AND-HOLD BOTTOM LINE

Despite its flaws, the buy-and-hold strategy offers individual investors the opportunity to achieve significant earnings over time. It does not guarantee you will make a profit or not lose money.

Buying wisely and having the courage to hang on through tough times is important to make the strategy work. Buy-and-hold will not turn a turkey into an eagle.

One danger of the strategy is a strict adherence no matter what. That doesn't make sense. Hold on if the stock drops but nothing has fundamentally changed about the company, but if the "great" company loses its greatness, move on to some other stock.

PRICE FOLLOWERS

A strategy that might be called the opposite, although not an exact opposite, of the buy-and-hold adherents is focused on hitting certain stock prices to drive buy and sell actions.

Caution

> Don't fall into the trap of buying on price alone. Just because a stock is down significantly doesn't mean it's a bargain.

These folks study a stock and arrive at a price they believe is a fair market value for the stock. They don't buy until they get that price. At the same time, they set a selling goal. Once the stock hits this mark, they either sell or put in escalating sell limit orders to protect the price.

This strategy has two premises: The first is that the way to build a portfolio is to never take a big loss. The second is that once a stock reaches a certain price, the market has overvalued it and you should sell before the market corrects the price (the price falls).

There is no arbitrary hold time on the stock. You act when the stock hits the appropriate price. This tends to take some of the emotion out of the process.

PRICE-SETTING: PROS

This strategy has an almost mechanical quality about it, since you operate with an established plan from the beginning. There is no emotion in the decision to buy or to sell.

If you cut your losses before they get too big, you preserve capital for other investments. Allowing your profits to rise until a certain retreat (say a 10 percent drop in price) puts no limits on your potential return.

This conservative strategy is happy with small losses and slightly larger gains.

PRICE-SETTING: CONS

Like all strategies, this one has some flaws. Moving in and out of stocks on minor price changes may knock you off a stock before you are ready.

This strategy is even more dependent on careful analysis than the buy-and-hold plan. You need the ability to determine a fair market price for the stock and a reasonable level to take profits. You are more likely to get big swings in price in the short run. These swings might cause you to sell too early or buy too high.

For example, if you won't accept a drop of more than 10 percent of the stock's price, you may sell prematurely. Volatile stocks may move that much and more in a single trading session.

Tip

Be sure you know how to use stops, stop limit orders, and other price-sensitive controls on your trading account before you make a mistake.

You could take a 10 percent loss on a stock, only to watch it turn around to take off without you. Practitioners of this strategy point out that it is also possible that 10 percent dip may turn into a 25 percent or more drop, which could take years to recover.

Another significant negative is the taxes and commissions you might incur with active trading. Any stock sold for a profit in less than one year faces ordinary income tax rates for your tax bracket.

DOLLAR COST AVERAGING

Should you dollar-cost-average your way through a bear market? It's arguable, but for the average investor (as opposed to the professional) it's still one of the best tools for building wealth in the stock market.

A key to this strategy is picking the right vehicle and, for most investors, dollar cost averaging is more convenient to use with mutual funds, which can automatically deduct a certain amount out of your checking account each month.

Tip

> Many mutual funds will dramatically lower the initial deposit if you agree to let them debit your bank account by a fixed amount each month.

Many independent Web sites rank mutual funds (I believe Morningstar.com is the best). It is easy to see how the fund is doing compared to an appropriate index or peer group with Morningstar.com tools. As long as the fund doesn't fundamentally change, stick with it through the down times when you are buying more shares with your fixed monthly deposit.

When the fund begins to rise, you are still there to participate in the growth. Trying to jump in and out of markets is too risky for most people.

TIME STRATEGY

Time is your investment's best friend. Time is why buy-and-hold works. Time will cover many investing mistakes.

The best thing you can do for yourself is start now, today, if you're not already an investor. If you start early enough (and there's no such thing as too early), you can make several mistakes along the way and still end up with a sizable nest egg at retirement.

Time defeats bear markets, too. Even though in the middle of one it may not seem like it, bear markets will pass. You want to be there when it happens and enjoy the upturn.

CONCLUSION

No single strategy is perfect or works for everyone. As you gain experience as an investor, adopt a strategy or devise one of your own. Whatever you decide, it needs to make sense to you and meet some basic investing guidelines. This strategy will carry you through bear markets with much less anxiety.

CHAPTER 20

DIVERSIFY OR DIE

Diversification is the process of spreading your assets over a number of different asset classes and different maturities to prevent a portfolio overloaded in one area from dragging down all of your holdings.

Unfortunately, diversification is not nearly as sexy as investing in Internet/tech stocks. You won't hear many people standing around the water cooler bragging about fine-tuning their portfolio by adding an international stock fund. I haven't seen any reports on how many people took money out of other investments to dump it into the Internet/tech craze of the late 1990s, but I'll bet there were a lot of them.

If you had a well-diversified portfolio going into the hottest part of the bull market, you didn't do as well as those folks who rolled the dice on Internet/tech stocks. It would have been difficult to not make money during that feeding frenzy.

Caution ————————————————————————

Many investors who made money early in the 1990s bull market confuse luck with success. When the market began to unravel, luck was not enough to keep their heads above water.

What a difference a year makes in your perspective. The Nasdaq is down over 60 percent, and the Dow and S&P 500 have suffered significant blows. All of this happened in a year beginning in April 2000. The person with the well-diversified portfolio probably had a good run during the bull market, but their return looked anemic compared to the Internet/tech investor.

In previous chapters, we discussed diversification and asset allocation as ways to defend against a bear market. In this chapter, we are going to spend additional time on diversification. Specifically, we'll look at how you can classify a number of different assets and suggest how they may or may not fit into your portfolio. Think of them as pieces of a puzzle that has no single solution. You can put them together in many different ways to achieve your goal.

In the next chapter, we will look at using these pieces in defining the asset-allocation model that is right for you.

PUZZLE PIECES: STOCKS

Diversification is the process of spreading your assets over different types and maturities of investments. Asset allocation is precisely defining what proportion each asset represents in your portfolio.

Another way to think of diversification is like the ingredients in a recipe: eggs, milk, sugar, flour, and so on. Asset allocation is the recipe itself: two eggs, one cup of milk, a cup of flour, and so on.

Some folks treat diversification and asset allocation as two terms with the same meaning. Even though I draw a distinction, it's just for clarification. You may read information on diversification that sounds just like what I call asset allocation. Don't be put off by the semantics. It's the process that's important, not what I call it.

Tip

Classifying stocks by a single system makes it easier to compare similar issues when looking for an investment.

When we looked at asset allocation in earlier chapters, it was in the context of stocks, bonds, and cash (either individual instruments or mutual funds). We talked about them in some broad terms, like large cap, growth, value, and so on.

Stocks don't lend themselves to easy classification, but a number of Web sites do this for you. Using their system, you can discover whether a stock fits a growth or aggressive model. My favorite system is from Morningstar.com. It classifies stocks into eight types based on financial measures of growth, profitability, and so on. You can use their system to help identify components of your asset-allocation model. If you're looking for an aggressive growth stock, Morningstar will help you identify those stocks that fit that type, then you can choose the stock that best fits your needs from a much smaller subset than the whole market.

If you don't have Internet access at home, try your public library. Most libraries offer free access to the Internet and may have personnel to help you get started. For those readers without access to the Internet, here are some definitions that will roughly track with some of Morningstar's stock types. My definitions are helpful, but Morningstar's are much more precise and worth the effort to research potential stock buys.

Tip

If you haven't taken the plunge into the Internet, I strongly encourage you to. It's not as expensive or complicated as you might think. You don't have to trade online, and the access to free information is unbelievable. I can't imagine today's investor buying and selling without access to Internet research.

AGGRESSIVE GROWTH STOCKS

These companies exhibit rapid growth in sales and—hopefully—earnings over an extended period. Many people considered the new Internet/tech stocks aggressive growth, but most of these wonders failed the earnings test. Without earnings, you're still dealing with a company in the startup mode.

Many aggressive growth stocks don't pay dividends; instead, they push profits back into the company to finance more growth. These companies can put up big growth numbers and impressive increases in stock prices, but they are also very sensitive to economic slowdowns.

If an aggressive growth company issues a warning that they won't hit revenue or earning projections, investors are likely to dump them. Consequently, aggressive growth stocks tend to be volatile. Often these stocks lead the market into a bear and lead the market out. Look for growth rates in excess of 20 percent in revenues and a strong quarter-to-quarter increase in earnings. Be very careful that these stocks don't dominate your portfolio after a big run-up in the market.

GROWTH STOCKS

Much lower numbers in revenue growth distinguish growth stocks from aggressive growth. However, growth stocks can be cash machines with earnings that are rising at a good clip. These companies are established and confident in their place in the economy. They pay out more of their earnings in the form of dividends (or stock buy-backs) than aggressive growth firms do.

Tip

> You can't afford to not have some part of your portfolio in growth assets. You have little opportunity to participate in an upward movement in the market without growth stocks or mutual funds.

Growth stocks are a key part of any diversification strategy with the exception of the radically conservative. They still have growth potential, but are less likely to exhibit wild swings in price.

As growth firms mature, they show slower and slower growth, but they may pay out increasingly high dividends. Folks who can use current income (retirees, for example) and some stability of price favor these stocks. Their steady dividends help offset a decline in price during a bear market. The company isn't likely to grow significantly, but it's steadiness is ideal for investors who want some security of principal and income.

HARD ASSET STOCKS

This type corresponds directly to the Morningstar stock type. These companies are involved in such enterprises as the following:

- Mining, especially precious metals
- Real estate
- Timber

Stock in these companies typically represents a hedge against inflation since they tend to move differently from the market. You might consider a hard asset stock as a temporary hedge; however, they are not exempt from the effects of recession.

VALUE STOCKS

Value stocks represent potential bargains in the market. They represent companies that are, for some reason, out of favor with the market. The companies may be distressed or just in industries that don't have the growth potential of other sectors. Distressed companies may be turnaround possibilities or just poorly run firms that are going nowhere fast.

C a u t i o n

> Some stocks are values because the company is a loser. Buying cheap doesn't mean the stock will automatically rise at some point. More cheap stocks stay that way than rise to new highs.

The market undervalues value stocks. A low P/E relative to the rest of the market or industry peers is one sign of a value stock. Value stocks can occupy a small part of the aggressive side of your asset-allocation model. They are aggressive because there is a chance the stock will not move up during a bull market, and you will lose the opportunity for growth.

Value stocks don't do much for your diversification goal. You want components of your portfolio to move when other parts are not. Value stocks seldom react strongly to the market.

THE BOTTOM LINE ON STOCKS

Using a consistent system for identifying stock types is a good way to fill in your asset-allocation model with the proper asset. Morningstar.com's stock types are comprehensive tools that can help you compare stocks using the same criteria.

T i p

> In the interest of complete disclosure, I have no financial interest in Morningstar.com, and they in no way compensate me for my opinions.

PUZZLE PIECES: MUTUAL FUNDS

Mutual funds are even harder to classify for the do-it-yourself investor unless you have access to the Internet. The major problem with mutual funds is that their name may or may not say something about how and where they invest your funds. When you are filling in an asset-allocation model and need an aggressive growth fund, it doesn't help to find out the fund you picked routinely keeps 30 percent of its investments in cash. Although you may find the reading difficult, it is always a good idea to read a fund's prospectus regarding investment strategies and goals. Ultimately, you define a mutual fund by where it invests your money, regardless of what the fund names itself.

Morningstar.com has an extremely helpful system for classifying mutual funds. They classify every individual stock by a number of financial ratios such as growth, value, and so on; look at which stocks the mutual fund buys; and, from this mix, determine where the fund belongs in its classification system. Morningstar also ranks funds by growth types, risk, and a number of other categories. The site also allows you to look at the individual stocks in each fund to make sure you are not buying two funds with essentially the same companies.

Many mutual-fund holders found themselves in this fix when the Nasdaq took its 2000–2001 dive. Investors discovered that they owned several funds that were each heavy in the same Internet/tech stocks. This defeats the whole purpose of diversification.

Tip

> Mutual funds offer many investors the best way to participate in the market because they can turn most of the decision-making over to professionals.

Another great piece of information on mutual funds is how much they have invested in various economic sectors and a rating on how well they might hold up in a bear market. If you don't have access to Morningstar.com or some other free Internet-based service that classifies mutual funds, I would suggest you use a broker that can get this information for you. Without this information, you may or may not accomplish the goal of diversification—you won't know for sure until it is too late and the market punishes you.

PUZZLE PIECES: BONDS

You cannot consider your portfolio diversified without some bonds in the mix. You can use individual bonds or a bond mutual fund to meet this goal. Bonds add stability to your portfolio by fixing a return (for individual bonds) and often moving in different directions from the equities markets.

Investors use bonds in diversification to offset some of the instability in stocks. Bonds react to economic changes (interest-rate changes, in particular), but there seldom are the massive sell-offs that mark the stock market during a bear attack.

Investors caught in the frenzy of a charging bull market may be tempted to pull money out of bonds and put it where the growth potential is much higher. This defeats the purpose of diversification and, if a bear market catches you with your diversification pants down, could cost you dearly for the opportunity.

Tip

> If you feel yourself being caught up in the buying frenzy of a bear market, cut yourself off from the media hype for 48 hours. Don't watch television or listen to radio reports about the market. Stay off the Internet and avoid magazines with raging bulls on the cover. Out of the hype-storm, you may feel differently about that stock you just couldn't live without two days ago.

STICK WITH YOUR PLAN

The purpose of diversification is to achieve reasonable gains in the current market, while protecting your portfolio during a bear attack. Had a bear attacked one asset in the original model shown above, the investor would not have suffered near the loss chasing the fast dollars of runaway tech stocks. Taking cash out of other assets and putting it in the tech stocks compounded the mistake. That action alone caused the notion of diversification to vanish. The higher the tech stocks went, the worse the model became out of balance.

It's hard to resist the temptation to jump on the express train to wealth that a red-hot sector looks to be. How embarrassing is the water cooler talk when your associates find out you aren't dumping everything you own into the "sure-thing du jour"?

Maintaining diversification and fine-tuning it with asset allocation requires discipline and a commitment to long-term success. If you must speculate, do so outside your normal investment and retirement accounts.

However, consider this: The $10,000 you lose speculating would have grown to over $89,000 in 20 years if your portfolio earns 11 percent (not counting taxes). Of course, you aren't going to lose are you?

C a u t i o n
> Built into the collective consciousness of our society is a fascination with getting something for nothing or making a financial killing with no effort. That's not investing—that's the lottery.

Those investors who watched the Internet/tech skyrocket in the late 1990s understand how hard it was to not jump into that market with both feet. There were investors who did just that and sold off enough to get their money back and then some before the bubble burst. Yet, these folks were in the minority. With stocks going from nothing to triple digits almost overnight, it was difficult to convince yourself to stay diversified, especially when other sectors were flat or down.

Bear markets have voracious appetites. They enjoy nothing better than a good feeding of wealth. As we discussed earlier, the bear market in the Nasdaq of 2000–2001 (and counting) ate well over $2 trillion in wealth. That wealth is gone, and it won't come back. The surviving companies may rebuild some of that wealth, but it will take much longer than in the bull market preceding the fall. A well-diversified portfolio maintained a significantly higher value than the Internet/tech stock dominated accounts.

Of course, the story of the bear that ate the Nasdaq isn't just about out-of-whack portfolios. It's a larger tragedy of investors who only invested in the Internet/tech-stock boom. While the media (both Internet and traditional) have to take some blame for the superhype surrounding the market, no one pointed a gun at investors and made them buy tech.

WHY SLOW AND STEADY WINS THE RACE

I could make a lot more money writing books with titles like *Become a Millionaire in 30 Days Trading Penny Stocks with Borrowed Money*. Of course, if I could actually do that, why would I want to write a book about it?

T i p

> Focusing on a diversified portfolio is the best way to keep common sense in your investing. You will thank yourself in 20 years when your portfolio has continued to grow year after year.

Investing is not a get-rich-quick scheme, but that's just what it became at the height of the Internet/tech-stock boom. The daytraders and IPO hawks filled the media with stories of easy money that was lying around waiting for you to grab.

Quick profits are a powerful narcotic. Even after the massive sell-off in Internet/tech stocks, investors are still looking for the good old days of triple digit Nasdaq gains. One mutual-fund official told me that even though their tech fund was down 70 percent and still falling in March 2001, people were putting new money into the fund. His sense was that at least some of these investors expected the sector to shoot back up any time and resume its climb to 10,000.

That may or may not happen. While the die-hard tech investor is still waiting for the market to come back, the slow-and-steady investor with a well-diversified portfolio continues to make money month after month.

IT TAKES COURAGE TO STAY DIVERSIFIED

The hardest thing an investor can face is a charging bear. The second hardest thing is a bull charging away from you. Both situations require courage to stay diversified. Unfortunately, the common reaction to either situation is to jettison the diversified portfolio in favor of a pure defensive strategy or an offensive charge to catch up with the bull.

Even if investors don't lose complete control, there is a tendency to overreact to rapidly changing market conditions. You may want to dump anything aggressive in your portfolio in favor of bonds or cash. If you have a diversified portfolio, you won't have a huge position in aggressive assets, with the possible exception of very young investors.

When a bear market heads your way, reexamine your portfolio to make sure you know all your aggressive positions (no unknown aggressive asset buried in mutual funds). Unless you have a high aversion to risk, keep your portfolio balanced with some aggressive assets (growth stocks, mutual funds, and so on).

When the market turns around, it will almost certainly be the growth stocks that lead you out of the bear's mouth. If you're completely defensive, there won't be anything in your portfolio to catch the bull market on the way up. This puts you in the unfortunate position of trying to catch the train after it has left the station. Since we already established that you can't call the market bottom, you will miss the upturn until it's well on its way.

Remain in your diversified portfolio and you have a better chance at weathering the bear market and catching the upturn quickly.

CONCLUSION

Diversification means you may not profit to the fullest in certain bull markets. It also means you may not lose to the fullest in bear markets.

Maintaining a well-diversified market takes some effort, since major market moves can unbalance your portfolio. It takes courage to stay diversified when jumping into a hot sector seems like such easy money. However, in the end, you'll come out ahead with a steady return.

CHAPTER 21

YOUR WEAPON OF CHOICE

I hope by now I have convinced you that there are only two real weapons you can use to defend your portfolio from a bear attack: diversification and asset allocation.

Asset allocation is a way to target the precise defense you need. However, no matter how hard we try, some bears are just too powerful. Bears reinforced by recession, deflation, or inflation can be formidable enemies. When faced with this much strength, the best we can hope for is to keep damage to a minimum. It may not be much consolation to know that your portfolio is only down 20 percent while the market is off 40 percent. However, you have cut your potential loss in half, and that's worth celebrating.

Using diversification, you spread your assets over the market spectrum of conservative to aggressive. Asset allocation defines the specific amount of each asset as percentage of your total portfolio.

MONITORING ALLOCATION

It doesn't do much good to set up your asset-allocation model to protect your portfolio from bears if it becomes out of balance thanks to a large movement in the market.

> **T i p**
>
> It is important to stay on top of your asset-allocation model. If it becomes unbalanced, you have defeated the purpose.

Many folks during the bull market of the late 1990s may have had 10 percent of their portfolio in Internet/tech stocks before the explosion. When the dust settled, the tech sector of their asset-allocation model had increased to 30-plus percent. The huge run-up in tech stocks increased the total portfolio. However, when combined with taking money out of some other assets and putting more into tech, those stocks dominated the portfolio.

Here is what the model looked like originally, during the bull market, and after the crash.

Assets	Original Model		Bull Market Run-Up		After the Bear Bites	
Tech stocks	$10,000	10%	$43,000	34%	$5,000	6%
Other asset	$20,000	20%	$18,000	14%	$17,000	21%
Other asset	$20,000	20%	$18,000	14%	$15,000	19%
Other asset	$20,000	20%	$18,000	14%	$13,000	16%
Other asset	$20,000	20%	$18,000	14%	$17,000	21%
Other asset	$10,000	10%	$10,000	8%	$8,000	10%
Total:	$100,000	100%	$125,000	100%	$81,000	100%

As you can see, the choice to take money out of other assets proved to be very unwise. When the bottom fell out of tech stocks, the portfolio was devastated. What should the investor have done to prevent this disaster?

The choices weren't popular during the middle of the tech-stock boom. To bring the asset-allocation model back into balance, the investor must sell off tech stocks and redistribute the cash to other assets or add more money to other assets so the percentages got back in line. This would undoubtedly create some significant tax bills, and you may not have extra cash lying around to add funds to the other assets.

Tip

> You should always be mindful of the tax consequences in selling investments. However, don't let tax concerns stop you from taking actions to protect your portfolio.

Some investors who knew they were violating their asset-allocation model told themselves they would ride the Internet/tech stock boom until it reversed itself. They would sell for a fat profit, then wait until the tech stocks bottomed out and use some of the profits to pick up bargains among the devastated tech stocks.

A nice plan, however, investors in the middle of a boom might not give up so easily. They might convince themselves that every dip was merely a correction, and the stock would soon begin soaring to previous heights and more.

HARD CHOICES

Rebalancing your portfolio can be painful when one part is on a hot streak. Our natural tendency is to let profits run, but if you're truly concerned about protecting your portfolio, you will make the hard decisions. Another solution for our hypothetical portfolio above is to follow a simple rule: Never reduce a position in one asset to increase a position in another asset just to take advantage of a hot market.

Caution

> Selling assets to put the proceeds in a hot sector is gambling at best and dangerous at worst. Should a bear attack that sector, you will likely suffer major losses.

Obviously, as your goals and time horizon change, you will change assets and percentages of other assets. Just don't engage in this activity to put more money in a hot sector. These have a tendency to cool off—sometimes quite rapidly. Let's look at the portfolio after the bull market run-up.

Assets	Bull Market Run-Up	
Tech stocks	$43,000	34%
Other asset	$18,000	14%
Other asset	$18,000	14%
Other asset	$18,000	14%
Other asset	$18,000	14%
Other asset	$10,000	8%
Total:	$125,000	100%

This is a disaster waiting to happen. Our investor's first mistake was to pull money out of the other assets to add to the tech-stock sector.

The first thing he needs to do is cash in enough tech stock to get the other assets back up to their original levels ($2,000 from four assets for $8,000). Now the portfolio looks like this:

Assets	Bull Market Run-Up	
Tech stocks	$35,000	28%
Other asset	$20,000	16%
Other asset	$20,000	16%
Other asset	$20,000	16%
Other asset	$20,000	16%
Other asset	$10,000	8%
Total:	$125,000	100%

This looks better, but the tech stocks are still dominating the portfolio. In an almost perfect world, the investor would continue making the hard choices, reduce his tech stocks back to 10 percent of the portfolio, and redistribute the proceeds to the other assets.

Assets	Original Model		Bull Market Run-Up	
Tech stocks	$10,000	10%	$12,500	10%
Other asset	$20,000	20%	$25,000	20%
Other asset	$20,000	20%	$25,000	20%
Other asset	$20,000	20%	$25,000	20%
Other asset	$20,000	20%	$25,000	20%
Other asset	$10,000	10%	$12,500	10%
Total:	$100,000	100%	$125,000	100%

Now, when the bear attacks (and note that all assets are hit by the bear) the results are not nearly so bad.

Assets	Original Model		Bull Market Run-Up		After the Bear Bites	
Tech stocks	$10,000	10%	$12,500	10%	$1,786	2%
Other asset	$20,000	20%	$25,000	20%	$21,250	24%
Other asset	$20,000	20%	$25,000	20%	$18,750	21%
Other asset	$20,000	20%	$25,000	20%	$16,250	18%
Other asset	$20,000	20%	$25,000	20%	$21,250	24%
Other asset	$10,000	10%	$12,500	10%	$10,000	11%
Total:	$100,000	100%	$125,000	100%	$89,286	100%

The portfolio is still out of balance, but no single asset dominates it. When I applied the same percentage reductions in all assets, the loss in tech stocks did not have the dollar impact as when it dominated the portfolio. This maneuver saved the investor over $9,000 in losses, and all the assets except tech stocks are close to their original allocations.

Obviously, this is just an example of one strategy you could employ. Unfortunately, it requires the courage to sell off the tech stocks just when they're booming. This proved the correct strategy, but if the bull had continued for another six months, the investor would have missed even higher gains.

This bear launched an across-the-board attack and the portfolio didn't have a cash component, which would have offered another strategy.

Tip

> It is not wise to hide all your assets in cash accounts, because there will be nothing to take advantage of the market when it begins to rise out of a bear.

The investor could have sold off the tech stock like before, but instead of putting the money back into the other assets, he could have kept it in cash. In this bear market, that would have been the best solution. Everyone is a great investor when looking backward. The trick is to protect yourself going forward.

ANOTHER SOLUTION

If you simply can't stand to cash in a winning investment like the tech stocks in the previous section, there is another alternative. It also requires discipline and some attention to the market.

The first task is to sell off some tech stocks and return the other assets to their full funding. The next step is one you take in your head. Take all the gains out of the tech-stock sector of your asset-allocation plan. Mentally, you have rebalanced your portfolio, and you have a sum of money tied up in tech stocks that sits outside your portfolio.

If these are individual stocks, consider trading tools to protect your profit. You can use a "stop limit order" to set a price below the current price. If the stock falls to this point, the order becomes a market order, and the system automatically sells the stock.

T i p

> Protecting profits is not the same as market timing when done with a commitment to sell upon a specific retreat in price. This is letting the market time itself.

Should the stock(s) keep rising, you can raise your stop limit order accordingly. One way to visualize this process is to think of a ladder with rungs going up and down. As the stocks rise, you follow up the ladder with new stop limit orders.

That ladder might look like this:

ORIGINAL COST OF STOCK: $10 PER SHARE—1,000 SHARES

Price of Stock	Stop Limit Order
$20	$16
$24	$18
$30	$25
$35	$28
$42	$32

In this example, you will notice that there is an increasing spread between the stop limit order and the price of the stock. There are two reasons for this:

- First, at the lower price, the stock doesn't have to move much to take away your profit.

- Second, as the stock gets more expensive, it will likely become more volatile on daily trading. A lower stop limit order keeps you in the stock through corrections and still protects your profit.

This system requires you to keep a close eye on the market and move your stop limit orders up as necessary. However, you should never lower the stop limit order. When you do this, you are trying to time the market and could easily watch your profit disappear. Some investors use a percentage to figure their stop limit order. Either way, you are using logic and reason to set the price as opposed to hope and emotion.

Using stop limit orders is a way to let the market time itself. You are not attempting to call a market turn. You are setting a price and letting the market come to that price or move away from it. When the market backs up and you're cashed out of the tech stocks, take the cash and either reinvest per your asset-allocation model or put it in a cash instrument if you believe a bear market is lurking.

WHAT ABOUT MUTUAL FUNDS?

If all or a major part of your portfolio is in mutual funds, you face a different set of challenges. Regular mutual funds don't post intra-day prices like individual stocks. Mutual funds are "marked to the market" after trading on the stock exchanges has closed.

The share price, also known as net asset value (NAV), is a reflection of the performance of the fund's individual investments. After the market is closed, the fund readjusts the NAV to reflect the new individual values of its holdings. If you want to use the strategy of protecting your profits, you will need to watch the fund's NAV every day. Unlike stocks, there are no stop limit orders for mutual funds.

You can only tell the fund or broker that you want to redeem X dollars out of the account. Check the fund's prospectus for rules regarding redemptions relative to the market's close. This shouldn't be a real problem, just an inconvenience. Since mutual funds are by definition diversified (with the exception of some sector and index funds), they will usually not move in large increments from day to day. You need to set a share price that will be your sell order. When the fund hits that price or is close and moving in a downward direction, redeem your shares.

Tip —————————————————————————————————

Mutual funds are slightly harder to work with because you only get fresh pricing once a day. Usually, this is not a problem because mutual funds don't often move in big steps one way or the other.

Unfortunately, this system relies on your attention to the share price, unlike the strategy for stocks that use orders that execute automatically when the stock hits your stop limit order price. I suggest you write the price on a piece of paper and keep it where it will remind you to check the NAV. If you are riding a bull market up, you can change your sell price as often as necessary.

REBALANCING SCHEDULE

How often should you rebalance your portfolio? I would check it every month or so during a normal market and more frequently when the market is moving strongly in one direction or the other. It's probably not necessary to rebalance if one or more assets are only a few points off target. However, watch for bracket creep if one sector is growing faster than the rest of the market.

If there are signs of economic slowdowns or bear markets in the near future, reevaluate your portfolio to see if you want to take a more conservative stance until the uncertainty is over. In Chapter 13, "Age-Appropriate Strategies," I discussed the components of conservative asset-allocation models. Your two most important conservative or defensive tools are cash and bonds. Inflation on the horizon signals interest rate increases, which aren't going to be good to bonds. Cash will be a better choice. A looming recession means interest rates are likely to drop, which will help bonds and not cash.

Caution ──

> Keep an eye on the Fed through the media for hints of whether interest
> rates are likely to go up, stay the same, or go down.

Avoid making major shifts in your portfolio in response to possible economic or market problems. Your portfolio should stay balanced regardless
of bulls or bears.

USE OF CASH

I believe cash should be a part of your asset-allocation model, although
you will undoubtedly see articles on asset allocation that don't mention
cash. There are reasons for eliminating cash from the model, one of the
most common being that cash instruments (CDs, money market accounts, money market mutual funds, and so on) are savings vehicles, not
investments. Rather than quibble, I would simply point out that cash in
a money market mutual fund earning 5 percent looked pretty good in the
bear-ravaged early months of 2001.

Opponents might argue that bonds and bond mutual funds can accomplish many of the same tasks as cash. I would beg to differ. Bonds
may not sell at par (face) value on the open market if interest rates have
risen. Bond mutual funds can actually lose part of your principal.

Neither of these is true of cash. Cash is always quickly convertible
to other assets, while the same isn't necessarily true.

In the previous section, we looked at what happens when a major
market move unbalances your asset-allocation model. A possible solution
was to sell off the inflated tech stock sector and put the proceeds into cash
instruments. Hiding in cash is not always the best answer. The biggest
downside is that when the market turns, you are not in a position to take
advantage of the earliest moves.

IRRATIONAL EXPECTATIONS

One of the biggest obstacles to accepting the structured approach to investing that asset allocation imposes is the irrational expectation still
smoldering after the Internet/tech-stock bull market. The frenzy built up

around the Nasdaq was just short of a riot. Unbelievable gains became believable and even expected. If the Nasdaq Composite didn't post a triple digit gain, pundits considered it a down market.

These expectations have long lives, even after the bull became hamburger. Investors are always looking to the unknown future. Could we see a return of the wild bull market in tech stocks? No one knows for sure, but that won't stop the true believers from loading up on downtrodden tech stocks in anticipation of a renewed buying frenzy.

Biotech stocks were once the objects of these same irrational expectations. Investors bid the stocks up, then when products and profits appeared to be years away, the market cooled and the sector collapsed. I am sure there are some folks who loaded up on these stocks hoping for a return to the center ring. One day, the market may prove them right.

T i p

Investors should not write off the Internet/tech stocks because of the 2000–2001 bear market. Survivors may be good buys now that the bear has punctured the hype.

The Internet/tech companies that survived the shakeout are not going away. They will continue to play a major role in our economy for years to come. Will they ever return to the boom days of the 1990s? No one knows for sure. However, I wouldn't dismiss the industry leaders. They will likely lead the way out of bear markets for several years to come.

ASSET-ALLOCATION TOOLS

As I noted earlier, I find the information and tools on Morningstar.com to be top rate for free services. In this final section, I want to introduce you to two tools that can be extremely helpful in guarding your portfolio from a bear attack, help you decide which mutual funds fit your asset-allocation model, and help you judge the likelihood of a portfolio's success.

PORTFOLIO ALLOCATOR

Morningstar's Portfolio Allocator is a tool that helps you decide which stocks and funds should go into your asset-allocation model. You set up the criteria for your model and the Portfolio Allocator suggest different mutual funds that might fit your model. These are funds selected from small groups of funds that Morningstar's analysts have studied in detail.

If you want the Portfolio Allocator to include individual stocks, you must manually enter them yourself. The Allocator looks at all the possibilities and reports the best combinations. The Allocator isn't giving advice, it is simply recommending a mix based on your input. The ultimate responsibility is yours.

Tip

The Internet has many good tools to help you with your investing questions and problems; however, always consider the source of the information before acting on it.

This tool is a very helpful starting place if you are a beginner in asset allocation. Don't use it as a recommendation service. It works by giving you a starting place, which is sometimes the hardest part.

THE GOAL PLANNER

Morningstar's Goal Planner is a helpful tool that estimates the chances of success in reaching a financial goal. You can enter your portfolio and the parameters of the goal (time to goal, amount, and so on). The Goal Planner shows you a graphic that plots the chances of your portfolio's success. The Goal Planner will also take a financial goal and let you adjust the percentages of cash, bonds, large cap stock, small cap stock, and foreign stock.

The tool uses a sliding graphic that allows you to adjust the percentages, and you can see the results (chance of success) on a chart. This is very helpful in understanding how the mix of assets changes the chances of success. Obviously, this tool can't predict the future, but it does give you a very educated guess at what results your portfolio might achieve in the future.

CONCLUSION

Asset allocation is your weapon of choice in defending your portfolio against bear attacks. Monitoring your allocation can force you into some hard choices when your portfolio needs rebalancing. Selling winners is often painful; however, leaving your portfolio out of balance is extremely dangerous. Bears love to attack undefended portfolios.

Rebalancing your portfolio after a strong market movement is necessary for it own protection. Check your portfolio once a month or more if the market is unstable. There are numerous tools on the Internet to help you establish an asset-allocation model and maintain its balance.

CONCLUSION

Now that you've worked your way through this book, I'm sure you're feeling supremely confident about handling any market emergency. Right?

Of course you're not. Wrestling with bear markets and a tumbling economy is unnerving at best and terrifying at worse.

However, there are steps—and now you know them—you can take to prevent the market from washing your portfolio wherever the bear wants to take it. The two words to keep repeating are: asset allocation.

This strategy prepares your portfolio to deal with the curve balls bear markets can throw. Will it guarantee you won't lose money? No, but it will give you a fighting chance to ride out a bear market with much less damage than a randomly constructed basket of investments. Ask anyone who had 40 percent of their portfolio in Internet/tech stocks what a bear market can do in a short period. (Maybe you were one of the victims.)

Asset allocation aims for the best return in today's market with reasonable protection against bear attacks. The key features you need to remember about bear-proofing your investments are …

- You must diversify your portfolio across stocks, bonds, and cash.

- How you determine the proportions for each asset depends on your time horizon, risk tolerance, and financial goal.

- In most cases, it doesn't make much difference if you use individual instruments or mutual funds to fill your asset-allocation model.

- There are signals that warn of upcoming economic and market turmoil.
- Investing always involves an element of risk. This is the question you must ask: "Is the potential reward worth the amount of risk involved?"
- Market timing is a dangerous and, ultimately, a losing game. Professionals can't do it and neither can you.
- A lot gets written about when to buy which stocks and mutual funds, but knowing when to *sell* is equally important.
- The underlying economic conditions (recession, inflation, or deflation) change the characteristics of bear markets and how you handle them.
- Bear markets can dramatically change retirement plans. Extra care is required when you approach or enter retirement to guard against bear attacks.
- There are definite signs that can tell you the difference between a bargain and a turkey investment in a bear market.
- Dollar cost averaging is the most effective investment tool most investors can use. It works in bear and bull markets.
- Rebalance your portfolio after major market moves.

These points will help you face bear markets with a greater confidence in your ability to make good decisions. You may not avoid a loss, but when the dust clears, your portfolio will look a lot healthier than if you acted like the good times would last forever.

GLOSSARY

This glossary contains definitions of common investment terms used in this book, plus a few more for good luck.

401(k) plan   A qualified, defined contribution plan offered by employers. It allows employees to have a certain percentage of their salary deducted and invested in the plan. The deduction is pre-tax, which reduces current income tax. The plan usually offers five to seven mutual funds among which the employee can distribute his deduction. In some cases, the employer may match a portion of the employee's contribution. The deposits and earnings are tax-deferred until withdrawn in retirement.

403(b) plan   Similar to the 401(k) plan, the 403(b) is for religious, educational, and other nonprofit groups. This plan uses tax-deferred annuities as investment vehicles.

actively managed mutual fund   Actively managed mutual funds meet their investment objectives by actively buying and selling securities. These funds may have high expense ratios and create tax liabilities passed through to the investor.

administrative fees   Fees charged by the mutual fund company to maintain and administer the fund.

annual report   A required document all publicly traded companies, including mutual funds, have to produce. It presents the financial results for the past fiscal year, audited by an accredited accounting firm.

asset allocation   The process of distributing your investment assets across stocks, bonds, and cash. This allocation will change as your life circumstances change.

bear market   A market where there are significant and long-term declines in market value as shown by falling market indexes—usually 20 percent or more.

blue-chip stocks The most prestigious and solid companies on the market. The term came from the fact that blue chips in poker are the most expensive ones.

bond mutual funds These invest in bonds and may target long or short maturities and different issuers. Triple tax-exempt bond funds are sold in specific states where residents may enjoy tax-free income from the bond fund.

bonds Debt instruments that represent an obligation on the part of the issuer to repay the debt. Governments and private corporations may issue bonds.

bull market A market characterized by significant and long-term growth in value in the stock market as shown by rising market indexes.

buy-and-hold investment strategy A strategy that suggests that buying and holding quality investments for long terms results in superior returns.

capital gain The profit from the sale of an asset; realized when you sell a stock or bond for a profit and when a mutual fund does the same. Mutual funds pass capital gains to shareholders. Any asset sold for a profit and held less than one year is subject to ordinary income tax by the owner. An asset held for more than one year and sold for a profit is a long-term capital gain, and the tax is 20 percent.

cash equivalents Financial instruments that represent a deposit of cash. They include certificates of deposits, money market accounts, and savings accounts. They are highly liquid.

certified financial planner A professional designation for someone who has extensive training in financial planning. Many certified financial planners charge a fee only for their services, while others may take a commission on products they recommend you buy.

closed-end mutual fund A hybrid type of investment that offers shares for sale only once. After that, there are no new shares sold. The remaining shares trade like stocks and can be bought and sold on the open market.

commissions Fees brokers charge to buy or sell securities for you.

common stock The primary unit of ownership in a corporation. Holders of common stock are owners of the corporation with certain rights, including voting on major issues concerning the corporation. Shareholders, as they are known, have liability limited to the value of stock they own.

compounding   The mathematical means by which interest is earned on the principal during one period, and then the next period the account earns interest on the resulting principal plus interest in the first period.

correction   A polite term for a full-scale retreat by a market sector or the whole market. It usually only lasts for a short time before reversing.

day trader   Someone who engages in aggressive trading using an Internet connection to a broker or a terminal in the broker's office. Day traders may make dozens of trades each day with the hope of making numerous small profits.

depression   A long-term (multiple years) decline in the national standard of living.

diversification   The calculated spreading of your investments over a number of different asset classes. This cushions your portfolio if one part is down, since different asset classes (stocks, bonds, cash, etc.) seldom move in the same direction. In mutual funds, you achieve diversification by the fund owning 50 stocks instead of a few.

dividend reinvestment plans (DRIPS)   These allow stock and mutual fund owners to reinvest dividends back into the investment program. You can also set up a DRIP and make periodic payments as a way of buying stock without going through a broker.

dividend yield   Calculated by dividing the current price per share into the annual dividend per share. The resulting percentage tells how cheap or expensive a dividend is relative to the stock price.

dividends   Portions of a company's profits paid to its owners, the stockholders. Not all companies pay dividends. The board of directors makes that decision. Companies that do not pay dividends reinvest the profits back in the company to finance additional growth.

dollar cost averaging   An investing technique that makes regular deposits in an investment account regardless of market conditions.

Dow Jones Industrial Average   Also known as the Dow, this index is the best known and most widely quoted in the popular press. The Dow consists of 30 companies considered leaders in their industries. Together, they account for a significant amount of the value of the market. Although not as reflective of the whole market as other indexes, the Dow is watched earnestly.

economic indicators Key measures of the economy's health, such as unemployment, wages, prices, and so on, that gauge the health of the economy.

economic risk The danger that the economy could turn against your investment. An example would be a real estate company in a period of high interest rates.

economics Pertains to the production, distribution, and consumption of goods and services, and the factors such as taxes, inflation, labor, and so on, that affect the economy.

equity What remains after paying all liabilities. Equities are another name for stock and indicate an ownership position.

expectation bubble The value added to a market or stock by investors who expect growth to continue on a straight line upward. They are willing to pay a premium for this future benefit, even if the benefit is in their imagination.

Federal Reserve Board Also known as "the Fed," it controls the nation's interest rates by setting the key interest rates charged to banks. Alan Greenspan has headed the board for many years. An unanticipated change in interest rates will have a dramatic effect on the markets. Raising and lowering interest rates is analogous to turning up or down the heat while cooking.

fiscal year The bookkeeping year for a company. It may or may not correspond with the calendar year.

focused funds These concentrate their investments in specific, narrow sectors of the market. The idea is to take advantage of rapid growth in the sector. The downside is that when the sector tanks, so does the fund.

full-service brokers Brokers who offer comprehensive services to persons wishing to invest, including recommendations on specific products and proprietary research.

fundamental analysis A method for evaluating a stock on the basis of observing key ratios and understanding the underlying business.

going public The process of taking a privately owned company and offering shares of stock to the public.

growth investment strategy A strategy that identifies companies with significant growth potential and is willing to ride out frequent market fluctuations.

growth mutual funds   Funds that seek investments in stock of companies with potential of rapid and sustained growth.

growth stock   A stock that usually pays no dividends but puts profits back into the company to finance new growth. Investors buy growth stock for its potential price appreciation as the company grows.

income investment strategy   A strategy that identifies sources of immediate income, whether through income stocks or bonds.

income mutual funds   Funds that invest in stocks and bonds that provide high levels of current income.

income stock   Provides current income in the form of dividends. Utilities are income stocks because of the strong dividends many pay.

index   A way to measure financial activity. An index has an arbitrary beginning value and as the underlying issues change, the index either rises or falls.

index mutual fund   A fund that seeks to mimic some key market index like the S&P 500.

inflation   Too much money chasing too few goods, resulting in a sharp rise in prices without any extra value added, making money worth less. Inflation leads to rising interest rates and a cooling of the economy. If the economy slows down too quickly and too far, it may slip into a recession or even a depression.

initial public offering   The first time a company issues stock for sale to the public. The company is said to be "going public" when this happens. The offering is highly regulated and often surrounded by a lot of media attention.

intraday   Prices that occur within a single trading day for the same stock. Speculators and day traders follow them closely.

large cap stock   Any company with a market capitalization of $5 billion or more.

limit order   Instructs your broker to buy a stock when the price drops to the level you set.

limit order to sell   Instructs your broker to sell a stock when the stock climbs to a predetermined level.

liquidity   Refers to how easily a financial instrument can convert to cash. A mutual fund is highly liquid, while an apartment building would be highly illiquid.

loaded fund   A fund that charges a sales fee or commission. The load may be up front or deferred.

lost opportunity costs   When you cannot act on an opportunity because your money is locked in another investment or you pass up a chance for profits because fear or the lack of information holds you back.

management fee   Also called the investment advisory fee, charged by the mutual fund company and used to pay the fund's manager, who is responsible for making sure the fund meets its objectives.

market capitalization   A way of measuring the size of a company. You calculate it by multiplying the current stock price by the number of outstanding shares. A stock trading at $55 with 10,000,000 outstanding shares would have a market cap of $550 million.

market cycles   Periods of market ups and downs.

market indicators   A collective name for a number of indexes and other measurements of market activity.

market order   An order to buy or sell placed with your broker requesting the best price at that moment.

market value risk   The danger that your investment will fall out of favor with the market.

mid cap stock   Any company with a market capitalization of $1 to $5 billion.

money market accounts   Special savings accounts usually offered by financial institutions that pay a higher interest rate than regular savings but require a higher minimum balance. They are not the same as money market mutual funds.

money market mutual funds   Funds that invest in short-term money market instruments. You can often withdraw money on short notice without penalty. Some offer check-writing privileges.

mutual funds   Funds representing a group of individuals who have pooled their money and hired a professional management company to invest it for them. Each mutual fund has specific goals and objectives that drive its buy and sell decisions. Mutual funds may invest in stocks, bonds, or both.

Nasdaq   Also known as the over-the-counter market, it is the new kid on the block. Many of the companies listed here are fairly young, and this is the home of many of today's high-tech stars and former stars.

Nasdaq Composite Index Covers the Nasdaq market of over 5,000 stocks.

net asset value (NAV) The mutual fund equivalent of a share price. This is the price you pay when you buy into a mutual fund. Unlike stocks, mutual funds have no problems with fractional shares. Funds calculate the NAV subtracting the liabilities from the holdings of a mutual fund, then dividing by the outstanding shares.

New York Stock Exchange The oldest and most prestigious of all stock exchanges. The NYSE is home to most of the "blue-chip" companies.

New York Stock Exchange Index Covers all the stocks on the NYSE, making it a broad measurement of larger companies.

no-load fund A fund that charges no sales fees or commissions, either up front or deferred.

portfolio The collection of all your investment assets.

precious metals mutual funds Funds that invest in stocks and bonds of mining and trading companies of precious metals such as gold and silver.

preferred stock As the name implies, preferred stock is a different class of stock with additional rights not granted to common stock owners. Among these rights is first call on dividends.

price/earnings growth ratio (PEG) Looks into the future relationship of earnings and growth. You calculate the PEG by dividing forward earnings estimates into the P/E.

price/earnings ratio (P/E) A way to show how a company's earnings relate to the stock price. You calculate the P/E by dividing the current price of the stock by the annual earnings per share. The higher the P/E, the more earnings growth investors are expecting.

price-to-book ratio Taking the current stock price and dividing it by the book value per share calculates the price-to-book ratio. This relationship shows the value of the equity as it relates to the stock price.

prospectus A legal document potential shareholders of mutual funds and initial public offerings of stocks must have before they can invest. It lists complete financial details of the fund as well as the associated risks.

ratio Simply a comparison of the relationship between financial items. For example, price/earnings ratio shows the relationship between a company's earnings and its stock price.

real estate investment trusts (REITs)   Similar to mutual funds in that they are traded as securities, making them more liquid than other forms of real estate investments.

real estate limited partnership   Pools investors' money and buys income-producing properties.

recession   Marked by declining standards of living and rising prices. Officially, a recession is a decline in the nation's gross national product for two consecutive quarters.

return   Another way to say yield; a percentage.

risk   Measures the possibility that an investment will not earn the anticipated return.

risk tolerance   A way to judge how much risk you are willing to take to achieve an investment goal. The higher your risk tolerance, the more risk you are willing to take.

sector mutual funds   Invest in various sectors of the economy such as technology or healthcare.

Securities and Exchange Commission (SEC)   The chief regulatory body over the stock markets and publicly traded companies.

small cap stock   Any company with a market capitalization of $1 billion or less.

socially responsible mutual funds   Funds that invest in carefully screened companies that meet certain social or ethical standards.

Standard and Poor's   An investment research service that provides a number of market indexes including the S&P 500. They also provide a rating service for bonds.

Standard & Poor's 500 (S&P 500)   A weighted index of 500 of the largest stocks. It is the most widely used measure of broad market activity and is often the benchmark other investments are compared to.

stock mutual funds   Invest exclusively or primarily in stocks. The stocks may be broad-based or in one sector. They may include foreign as well as domestic stocks.

timing the market   Investors who try to pick a stock's low to buy and a stock's high to sell are timing the market. No one can consistently do this with any success.

trade   Refers to the buying or selling of stocks, bonds, mutual funds, and other financial instruments. Depending on the usage, it can mean a single transaction or refer to the total market (trading was heavy).

unit investment trusts   Another hybrid fund that buys a fixed portfolio of stock or bonds and never sells or buys any more.

value mutual funds   These look for companies the market is undervaluing for some reason with the hope that their fortunes will return and the stock will experience significant growth.

value stock   The market underprices a value stock for whatever reason. Often, a stock's only sin is not being a part of the current hot sector.

yield   The percent returned to stockholders in the form of dividends.

RESOURCES

In this appendix, you will find a list of Web and published resources to assist you in planning and implementing your investment program.

FINANCIAL PLANNING PROFESSIONALS

www.financialplan.about.com—A whole Web site devoted to financial planning from About.com.

www.amercoll.edu/—Background information about the designation "Chartered Financial Consultant" and other financial planning designations.

www.cfp.com—Information on choosing a certified financial planner (CFP) from the Certified Financial Planner Board of Standards.

www.planningpaysoff.org—Search the database of the International Association for Financial Planning to find a Financial Planning professional near you.

investmentclub.about.com/finance/investmentclub/mbody.htm—Investment clubs are a great way to get started in investing, and this is a site completely devoted to investment clubs.

FINANCIAL PLANNING SOFTWARE

www.zdnet.com/pcmag/features/finance—A review of Managing Your Money personal finance software.

www.computershopper.zdnet.com—Reviews of Microsoft Money, Managing Your Money Plus, Quicken Deluxe, and Kiplinger's Simply Money.

www.quicken.com—Order Quicken Deluxe, Quicken Home and Business, Quicken Suite, Quicken Personal Financial Planner, Turbo Tax, and other Quicken products.

INVESTMENT PUBLICATIONS

Alpha Teach Yourself Investing in 24 Hours, Ken Little—This book is a comprehensive overview of investing techniques and strategies. It covers all the information you need to get started or to review the basics.

The Intelligent Investor: A Book of Practical Counsel, Benjamin Graham—Benjamin Graham is one of the best-known value investors of all time. Graham advocates a simple portfolio and stock selection methods.

The Only Investment Guide You'll Ever Need, Andrew Tobias—Andrew Tobias is a well-respected financial counselor and stresses no-load mutual funds.

The Complete Idiot's Guide to Making Money with Mutual Funds, Alan Lavine and Gail Liberman—This guide is a great primer for getting you on track with mutual funds. It is easy to follow and full of information, including definitions and tips.

Beating the Street, Peter Lynch—Peter Lynch is a name that inspires awe on Wall Street for his successful investing strategies.

The Complete Idiot's Guide to Managing Your Money, Robert Heady and Christy Heady—A great consumer guide to managing your money, this book is easy to read and full of practical tips.

Motley Fool's You Have More Than You Think: The Foolish Guide to Investing What You Have, David and Tom Gardener—These guys are no fools when it comes to investing advice. This book shows you how to get started with a small amount.

Technical Analysis of Stock Trends, Robert D. Edwards and John Magee—The authors offer a comprehensive look at a technical analysis of stock movement.

MARKET INDICATORS

The following is a list of key market indicators:

Dow Jones Industrial Average (www.dowjones.wsj.com)—The oldest and best known of all market indicators, the Dow consists of 30 stocks representing the leading companies in their industries. Here is a list of the stocks that make up the Dow Jones Industrial Average as of April 2001:

Alcoa, Inc.	Intel Corp.
American Express Co.	International Business Machines Corp.

AT&T Corp.	International Paper Co.
Boeing Co.	J.P. Morgan & Co.
Caterpillar, Inc.	Johnson & Johnson
Citibank	McDonald's Corp.
Citigroup, Inc.	Merck & Co.
Coca-Cola Co.	Microsoft Corp.
DuPont Co.	Minnesota Mining & Manufacturing Co.
Eastman Kodak Co.	Philip Morris Cos.
Exxon Mobil Corp.	Procter & Gamble Co.
General Electric Co.	SBC Communications, Inc.
General Motors Corp.	United Technologies Corp.
Hewlett-Packard Co.	Wal-Mart Stores, Inc.
Home Depot, Inc.	Walt Disney Co.

Nasdaq Composite (www.nasdaq.com)—The Nasdaq is home to many of the high-flying, high-tech companies on the market today. This composite index reflects the top 100 stocks.

New York Stock Exchange Composite Index (www.nyse.com)—This index covers all the stocks traded on the New York Stock Exchange.

Russell 2000 Index (www.russell.com)—The Russell 2000 is a key indicator for how the nation's small companies are doing.

Standard & Poor's 500 (www.standardpoor.com)—The S&P 500 is the most widely used benchmark for the market by investment professionals.

ONLINE BROKERS

The authoritative source on online brokers is Gomez.com (www.gomez.com). They use fees, ease of use, and a number of other factors to rank online brokers. Here are some of the top-rated online brokers:

1. Charles Schwab (www.schwab.com)

2. E*Trade (www.etrade.com)

3. DLJdirect (www.djdirect.com)

4. Fidelity Investments (www.fidelity.com)

5. NDB (www.ndb.com)

6. A.B. Watley (www.abwatley.com)

7. My Discount Broker (www.mydiscountbroker.com)

8. American Express Brokerage (www.americanexpress.com)

9. Suretrade (www.suretrade.com)

10. Morgan Stanley Dean Witter Online (www.online.msdw.com)

RETIREMENT CALCULATORS

www.quicken.com—The financial software giant has a great site with plenty of aids, including this comprehensive retirement planning calculator at www.quicken.com/retirement/planner/js/.

www.retireplan.about.com—A complete site devoted to retirement planning.

www.interest.com—This calculator helps you figure the future value of money before and after retirement.

www.firstar.com/persfin/—FirstStar bank's calculator includes inputs for a second income in the household.

www.moneycentral.msn.com/articles/retire—MSN.com shows how much you can spend after you retire.

www.principal.com/—The Principal Financial Group discusses expenses after retirement.

RISK TOLERANCE

www.better-investing.org—An article discussing risk tolerance and how yours should affect your investment decisions.

www.cigna.com/retirement—A short risk-tolerance quiz will help you sleep better at night with your investment decisions.

www.scudder-u.working4u.com—Another quiz on risk tolerance and the role it plays in investing.

ROTH IRA

www.university.smartmoney.com—Online SmartMoney magazine (from *The Wall Street Journal*) has complete Roth IRA information.

www.fool.com/retirement.htm—The Internet wits from Motley Fool have sound advice for IRA shoppers.

www.familymoney.com—Family Money is a good site with lots of information about IRAs

SEP IRA INFORMATION

www.dainrauscher.com—Find out how much you can contribute to a SEP, SIMPLE IRA, or Keogh plan from Dainrauscher.com.

www.newyorklife.com—New York Life details the benefits of using a SEP IRA for retirement planning made easy.

www.bankrate.com—Bankrate.com helps you calculate your eligible SEP IRA contribution.

ww.irs.ustreas.gov/basic/forms%255Fpubs/pubs/p590toc.htm—IRS guide on setting up and maintaining a SEP plan.

STOCK EXCHANGES

American Stock Exchange—www.amex.com
Chicago Board of Trade—www.cbot.com
Chicago Board Options Exchange—www.cboe.com
Chicago Mercantile Exchange—www.cme.com
Kansas City Board of Trade—www.kcbt.com
Nasdaq—www.nasdaq.com
New York Cotton Exchange—www.nyce.com
New York Mercantile Exchange—www.nymex.com
New York Stock Exchange—www.nyse.com
Philadelphia Stock Exchange—www.phlx.com

STOCK SCREENING

Stock screening services make finding the right stock or mutual fund much easier. Here are three that are worth getting to know:

- Microsoft's site is comprehensive and easy to customize at moneycentral.msn.com.
- Marketguide's StockQuest is a powerful screening tool, but it takes a while to get used to at www.marketguide.com.
- Morningstar.com's stock and fund selectors are easy to use and do not overwhelm you at Morningstar.com.

STOCK TRADING GAMES

www.smartstocks.com—Play the market without risking any money.

www.game.etrade.com—E*Trade, the online broker, offers several different games.

www.stocktrak.com—Offers prizes for best performance in monthly games.

INDEX

ABOUT THE AUTHOR

Ken Little is a writer and an editor specializing in investing and personal finance subjects. He is the author of four other books on investing and the Internet including *Alpha Teach Yourself Investing in 24 Hours* (Alpha Books), *The Complete Idiot's Guide® to Investing in Internet Stocks* (Alpha Books), *10 Minute Guide to Employee Stock Options* (Alpha Books), and *How to Integrate E-Commerce into Your Existing Business* (written under contract for MightyWords.com). He also served as technical editor for *The Complete Idiot's Guide® to Online Personal Finance* (Alpha Books).

Until recently, he was the "Investing for Beginners" guide for About.com, where, among other duties, he produced a weekly newsletter. He has been the business editor of a major daily newspaper, the senior marketing officer for a major financial services organization, and the publisher of several magazines.